HAUNTED FIELD GUIDE SERIES I

FIELD GUIDE TO CHICAGO HAUNTINGS BY JIM GRACZYK

-A GHOST RESEARCH SOCIETY PRESS PUBLICATION-

This book is dedicated to my daughter Rachel . . . my family and the Ghost Research Society.

Thanks to Dale Kaczmarek and Troy Taylor for all the advice and taking the time to listen. Special thanks to Emma Smith and Eugene Bender for all those countless hours of reading and writing assignments, you are both truly great professors.

My mom and dad taught me to never give up and work hard toward your goals, and upon that this is one of my accomplishments. Thank you all for believing in me, and helping me to succeed.

To that very special someone who has put up with me throughout these many years, my heart is forever yours.

Original Cover Artwork Designed by
Larry Arnold (Author of "Ablaze")
ParaScience International
http://www.parascience.com

This Book is Published by
Ghost Research Society Press
P. O. Box 205
Oak Lawn, Illinois 60454
(708) 425-5163
http://www.ghostresearch.org

ISBN: 0-9766072-2-0

Printed in the United States of America

THE HAUNTED FIELD GUIDE SERIES

Welcome to the first book in the Haunted Field Guide Series that was created by Jim Graczyk. Ghost Research Society Press will be dedicated to providing the readers with these "field guides" to not only haunted places, but to ghost research as well. In the books to come, we will take you beyond the cities and provide detailed listings, maps and directions to haunted places all over the Midwest and America. The series plans to devote books to various types of ghost research, investigations and much more.

We hope you enjoy this new series and that you will journey with us in the future as we take you past the limits of hauntings in America and beyond the furthest reaches of your imagination!

Happy Hauntings!

CONTENTS

Introduction - 1

Tragic Events - 3

Southside Chicago Area - 44

Downtown Chicago Area - 59

Northside Chicago Area - 69

Chicago Suburbs - 82

Research Organizations & Useful Websites -106

Bibliography - 109

About the Author – 110

Index - 111

North of Madison Street		South of Madison Street	
Street Name	Block	Street Name	Block
Chicago Ave.	800	Roosevelt Rd.	1200
North Ave.	1200	Cermak Rd.	2200
Fullerton Ave.	2400	31st St.	3100
Belmont Ave.	3200	Pershing Rd.	3900
Irving Park Rd.	4000	47th St.	4700
Lawrence Ave.	4800	55th St. (Garfield)	5500
Bryn Mawr Ave.	5600	63rd St.	6300
Devon Ave.	6400	79th St.	7900
Touhy Ave.	7200	87th St.	8700
Howard St.	7600	95th St.	9500

West of State Street		East of State Street	
Halsted St.	800	South Park Ave.	400
Ashland Ave.	1600	Cottage Grove Ave.	800
Western Ave.	2400	Woodlawn Ave.	1200
Kedzie Ave.	3200	Stony Island Ave.	1600
Pulaski Rd.	4000	Jeffrey Ave.	2000
Cicero Ave.	4800	Yates Ave.	2400
Central Ave.	5600	Commercial Ave.	3000
Ridgeland Ave.	6400	Brandon Ave.	3200
Harlem Ave.	7200		

State Street is 0 East & West   Madison Street is 0 North & South

INTRODUCTION

There is a fascination with the spirit world, yet not all people will admit the existence. People are afraid of something out of the norm; they don't like to talk about things that are unknown. They prefer to talk to you one on one, hopefully nobody else will hear what they are talking about, otherwise they might be considered strange or even crazy. Yet, strange sightings, strange smells, strange lights, and unusual events seem to be played over and over again throughout these many locations.

Could this all be explained in some way? Maybe not, but yet certain places have had some serious events taken place whether its been a sudden accident, a murder, or just a favorite place someone liked to visit. How could a place have something paranormal going on? Who could be the cause of this paranormal activity? Science sure would not approve of this, since it could not be replicated in a laboratory at this time.

In turn, I decided to put together a field guide to those numerous hauntings here in Chicago. The field guide will provide a quick reference on the locations throughout the city and within an hours drive. The location will have an easy street reference to aid the reader, and a map is included in each section to help get your bearings. Some locations I have listed important things you might be interested in seeing, whether it be a grave or a tragic event. Most of the locations are marked on the maps; those are the ones I thought might be a little hard to find.

This Field Guide should be used as a companion to numerous books such as: Windy City Ghosts, Haunted Illinois, Chicago Haunts, Haunted Places the National Directory. I highly recommend reading those books so as the reader has the complete story and a true understanding of all the facts about a particular site.

I ask that you please respect the locations you visit, some are on private property, and you might need permission. Visit these locations as if visiting an unfamiliar place. I wish you the best of luck, take some pictures and video.

Happy Hauntings!

CHICAGO'S TRAGIC EVENTS
WHY THE WINDY CITY IS SO HAUNTED!

There are many things that have happened throughout Chicago's history that have made an impact on how we live today. I am talking about very serious tragic events in which many lives have been lost. These deadly events took place because somehow, we as a society forgot to take a precaution against them. They say we learn from mistakes we make, but the mistakes we made have cost many lives. I would like to look at a few of these tragic events and mention how we now take precautions that make a difference in our lives today.

OUR LADY OF ANGELS

The first event is the Our Lady of Angels Fire that occurred in 1958. Our Lady of Angels was a Catholic grade school that was located at 909 N. Avers. The school was built in a modest neighborhood where many ethnic groups lived, though it was predominantly Italian.

It was December 1, 1958, a cold but clear day in Chicago. In attendance at the school were approximately 1400 students, 9 lay teachers, and 20 nuns. All of them

 were housed in 24 classrooms, and in some of these rooms there were as many as 60 children. Obviously, overcrowding was as common then as it is today.

The school day was coming to a close and at approximately 2:30pm, as many articles have reported, a small fire reportedly started in the basement stairwell.

As some articles state, there were two boys who had just come back from emptying wastebaskets and reported to their teacher they had smelled something burning. Their teacher then went out into the hallway, only to find it filling with smoke. She then quickly walked over to a nearby room where she talked with another teacher. They decided they had better notify the principal's office. There was a rule that stated that the office, and Mother Superior, had to be notified before any alarm was sounded to avoid a panic.

Upon reaching the principal's office, she was informed that the principal was substituting in a classroom downstairs. The teacher ran back down the now smoke-filled hall to notify the other teacher, and both agreed to evacuate their classrooms. As soon as the students were down in the church, and in a safe area, both teachers ran for help. One teacher ran across the street to the convent, while the other made a dash to pull the fire alarm.

It was now 2:42pm and the first call was received by the fire department. This was also at the same time the fire alarm sounded. The fire had now been smoldering for only a few minutes but was already making its way up the rear stairwell and into the corridor of the north annex. It was too late for the alarm and far too late for to escape.

To make matters worse, the fire department was misdirected to the Our Lady of Angels parish at 3808 W. Iowa. Even though this is just around the corner from the school, important minutes were lost. During this time, the priests and neighborhood people had been trying to evacuate the building.

This task was nearly impossible due to the fact that the  fire had swept up the stairwell and also into the walls. As the fire made its way up to that second floor, it managed to get into the ceiling area. The ventilator grills filled with smoke and made the hallways inaccessible. Thick smoke and gases filled the corridors and the fire started to make its way down from the ceiling of the second floor.

The ceiling light fixtures and windows started to explode from the heat of the fire. The only way out of the building now was for the children and nuns to exit through the second story windows. Children had begun to leap even before the fire department arrived on the scene. There were just too many of them to catch as they jumped. Because of this, many didn't have a chance at all.

As the fire department arrived, they disregarded the proper procedures and called in the 5-11, which is one of the most serious calls any fire department can make.

The 5-11 that was called in also requested any available ambulances that the City had to offer. Fire trucks came from all parts of the area to help battle this blaze and more than 43 pieces of fire equipment arrived on the scene. There were firemen running everywhere trying to save the children and nuns, some using ladders while some just heroically stood there catching those who jumped. It took the fire department until approximately 3:45pm to bring this deadly fire under control.

After a little more than an hour after they began fighting the deadly blaze, firemen entered the second story classrooms. It was grim site to see. The flames had consumed everything in their path leaving nothing untouched. Rooms 208, 209, 210, 211 and 212 all contained burned bodies of children and nuns that had to be carried out.

The grim task of recovering bodies was started and firemen carrying stretchers started to emerge from the ruined building. Many parents watched in a state of fright because they didn't know if any of their children had survived. Some parents were fortunate to find their children wandering around the nearby street, while others had to search the seven hospitals that received the injured. For those who did not find their loved ones in one of those hospitals, the final stop was the county morgue.

As the night came to a close there were a total of 90 dead, 87 children and three nuns. The fire eventually claimed a total of ninety-two students and three nuns. A total of over one hundred sixty children were saved. Close to 100 people suffered some sort of injury while fighting this fire, including teachers, staff, firemen, and civilians. An investigation into the fire was made immediately.

There were fingers being pointed in all directions as to who would be blamed for this event. The church's pastor, janitors, school personnel, a candy storeowner, and the Archdiocese of Chicago were all being blamed in one way or another. Some countries even blamed the United States for not enacting tough fire codes to schools.

Investigators tried to piece together the scene, as it had been just moments before the fire. They found that the fire had been started in 30-gallon trash drum in the basement stairwell. The fire flashed up after the heat built up and caused a window to break. Stairwell steps were made of wood and the walls were coated with flammable paint. This in turn caused the heavy black smoke. The investigators found that the electrical and heating systems throughout the building did not cause the fire. So, it was assumed that it was possibly arson.

The inquest that was held could not find the fire's cause, let alone the person who might have started the fire. All that came out of the proceedings were some long recommendations that would make schools safer.

Some of these recommendations included having fire alarm boxes placed right outside the school, sprinkler systems, fire doors, and fire safe construction of new schools. The fire alarm also had to be directly connected to the fire department. There was even a suggestion to make sure the fire department had tall enough ladders. This was from one report that claimed some of the ladders on the scene were too short to reach the victims.

Even though it was determined that the fire had apparently started in the basement stairwell, no person has ever been formally charged with starting it. However in January 1962, Cicero Police questioned a 13 year-old boy about a couple fires that had been started in the neighborhood. They found that after they pressed the boy, he admitted to a long history of playing with fire.

He had started his first fire in his family's garage at the age of five. He had also told a polygraph examiner that he had started around 11 other fires in a couple of neighborhood apartment buildings. All of these fires were started in basement stairwells with matches and paper. The examiner then asked if the boy had started the fire at Our Lady of Angels, but he denied it. The test however showed that the boy was lying about this question.

After a precise question by the polygraph examiner that made the boy very uncomfortable, he finally admitted he did start the fire in hopes of getting a few days off from school. He also hated his teachers and principal, because they wanted to expel him from school. This was because he missed so many days of class and his behavior was not desirable in the classroom.

Eventually, the boy had an eight-page confession in which he described how he went about starting the fire. He talked about how he had gone to the bathroom, and made his way to the basement where he found the drum and tossed in a few matches. Once the fire started he ran back up to his room and acted as if nothing had happened.

When asked why he didn't tell anyone about starting the fire, he exclaimed his dad would have beaten him, and the police might have given him the electric chair if convicted.

The confession was later revealed in a closed hearing, but it was ruled inadmissible because it had been improperly obtained. In addition, as the boy was under thirteen years of age, it could not be tried as a felony case. The judge did however find him guilty of starting the other fires in Cicero and sentenced him to a home for troubled boys out of state.

There is little question that the confession that was obtained was genuine for it pointed to a number of clues that were not available to the public. They were things that only the suspect who committed the crime would have known. The boy described the stairwell and where and when the fire was possibly started. Investigators also noticed similarities between the apartment fires and the school fire too. The polygraph examiner was convinced that the boy was being truthful in his confession and did start the fire at the school.

The parishioners on the other hand, just assumed it was some sort of "Act of God." The building was rebuilt and stood there until 1999, when it was closed due to low enrollment. I'd like to add that there is nothing noted or that has been reported to indicate that the new building is at all haunted. It does make you wonder though, with such a high death loss and the number of children that were involved if an impression from this tragic event might linger.

The aftermath of the fire had caused the City of Chicago to amend chapter 78 of the Municipal Code to include "Schools." There were many things added to include:

1. Enclosing all the stairwells with fireproof construction and provide fire doors leading into them.

2. Provide fire doors at all corridors and room partition openings.

3. Require automatic fire sprinkler systems in all school buildings.

4. Provide approved automatic internal fire alarm systems that are linked directly to the Fire Department.

A couple of other changes also included lowering the window height and their ledges from 37 inches, so that children would have better access to them. Some of the fire victims were unable to climb to the windows to escape.

All of the simple little precautions that we have in our Chicago schools today were placed there due to this great disaster. This also prompted many schools throughout the United States to amend their State and Local fire Codes. A survey was conducted by the National Fire Protection Association that showed an estimated 68% of schools had done something to improve their fire safety after this disaster.

There is a memorial at Queen of Heaven Cemetery in Hillside where twenty-five of the fire victims are buried. It's located in section 18, at the fork in the road on the west side, a corner that is not too far off the Roosevelt Road entrance. If you get a chance, visit the site and I would recommend reading the two books I have listed below.

FURTHER READING:
To Sleep with the Angels, by Dave Cowan and John Kuenster (1996)
Great Chicago Fires by Dave Cowan (2001)

IROQUOIS THEATER
The second tragic event occurred back in December 1903. The Iroquois Theater Disaster was a terrible fire that should have never happened. The theater itself was constructed at such a speed that it took just four months

to build. There were corners that were cut and the place was considered by many as "a disaster waiting to happen".

It was another clear and sunny day, December 30, 1903. Though it was cold, it didn't keep the holiday crowd away from the theater. People came from all over the area, many from out-of-town. Everyone wanted to see the popular funnyman Eddie Foy.

The entertainment business back then was centered on vaudeville and plays were the thing to see. The current

play, *Mr. Bluebeard,* was going to be performed during an afternoon matinee. The theater could seat 1,600, which made it one of the largest in the country. The theater on this day was going to hold about two thousand people. Many of them would be left standing in the aisles. There were mostly women and children present, who were on the holiday break from school. Since it was a Wednesday afternoon matinee, few men were there, since most of them held jobs.

Some time shortly after 3pm, during one of the scenes, a spark was seen coming out from one of the stage lights, followed by some floating paper that was on fire. At first no one in the audience panicked, thinking it was all part of the act. Meanwhile though, several members of the cast had already made a run for the alley behind the theater.

Suddenly, the stage's alleged "fireproof" curtain came

rolling down, but it got stuck in the halfway position. As the curtain got caught, it fanned the flames out into the audience area. People now began to panic and started to make their way to the doors.

The front doors of the theater had been made with a clever design that allowed them to swing inward, not outward. As people packed into them, they were crushed because the doors could not be pulled open. Most of the side doors of the theater, for some reason, were locked on this day. The side doors had new steel gates, with a locking system that the public was unsure of how to use. There was a fireman on duty but he was insufficiently supplied with firefighting equipment. To make matters even worse, the track where the curtain ran up and down was made of wood. The curtain, rumor has it, was made of the cheapest material and chances are that it wouldn't have made much of a difference if it had been fully deployed in the "fireproof" position.

The blaze was brought under control in less than thirty minutes, once the Fire Department arrived on the scene. By then, tragedy had already struck. Many people, in an attempt to flee the fire rushed the doors, trapped the people in the front. Bodies upon bodies piled up in many areas of the building, many passing out from smoke inhalation and a lack of air. People tried to jump from the balcony to the main floor to escape the fire. Others had jumped out the side windows of the theater in an attempt to escape, only to hit the hard pavement. Of course, the first ones that jumped had seriously been hurt or had died. The rest of them landed on those that made the first attempt, and managed to survive the fall. More people perished as the fire broke out under an escape stairwell.

The number of victims peaked around five hundred seventy-one, although some say it was closer to six hundred people. At least another three hundred people were seriously hurt. Tragically, of those killed in the fire, about forty of them were schoolteachers within the City of Chicago. School was closed that following Monday in their remembrance.

The recovering of bodies took about five hours after the fire was put out. A number of bodies were stacked in the alley beside the theater and this is how the term

"Death Alley" came about. Many relatives came here to identify their loved ones. There were also numerous bodies taken to the eighth floor of Marshall Field's department store, which served as a temporary morgue.

There was nobody actually punished for the neglect of the building. Money and the right political connections bought the men freedom. One person that did manage to do jail time in connection to the fire was a tavern keeper. Some of the bodies were sent to his nearby tavern as a temporary morgue. He apparently was convicted of robbing the dead.

The theater was later rebuilt and reopened within a few short months. The building did manage to survive for a number of years but was eventually torn down in 1925.

The lot was built upon and housed a number of different things. At the present time it is the site of the Ford Center for Performing Arts. This building is truly extravagant and hosts top name billing. If the building site is haunted, the public doesn't know anything about it yet, and the state of Marshall Field's eighth floor is also unknown. As for the alley, nothing unusual has been reported to this date.

The aftermath of this dreadful fire brought about some mandatory changes to theaters that included those nifty **EXIT** signs and lights, outward-opening doors, automatic sprinklers, a fire alarm system, and flame-resistant scenery, props, and costumes. All of the changes that were made can still be seen today in modern theaters and can be traced back to that dreadful day back in December 1903.

GRIMES SISTERS

The 1950's were a time when the economy was making a change and the post-war babies were looking toward a better future. The Chicago area was dealt a devastating blow in 1955 with the Schuessler-Peterson boy's murders. The crimes remained unsolved into 1956 when another stunning crime occurred.

The holiday season was coming to end and the date was December 28, 1956. Barbara Grimes, 13, who was a seventh grader at St Maurice School and her sister Patricia Grimes, 15, who attended Kelly High School, were out of school for the holiday break and decided to head to the Brighton Theater to see Elvis Presley's *Love Me Tender*. The girls left their mother's home at 3634 S. Damen with only $2.15, just enough money to see the show and take care of any other expenses they might incur.

How they got to the theater, which was a short distance away is not known, but possibly by walking or taking the bus. Friends do report they saw them in line waiting for popcorn around 9:30pm that night. There was nothing wrong at that point, since both were observed laughing and playing around like normal kids. What happened after the movie let out about 11pm is uncertain.

Numerous people claimed to see them board an Archer CTA bus, heading east into the City. The same people also claimed see them get off the bus at Western Avenue. This is about a mile and a half from the theater, and possibly a halfway point between their house and the theater. Why they would get off the bus a mile from their house is still a mystery.

The girl's mother started to worry since the girls always were in around midnight. The time was about 2:15am when she decided to phone the police to report that the girls had not come home from the theater.

The police questioned numerous eyewitnesses and chased whatever leads they had to follow. The days turned into weeks and flyers were circulated in hopes of bringing this to a happy end. Many hoped the girls had just run away, though there was no apparent reason, and they would see that they were missed and would come home.

There was a report that a train conductor saw them up north by Great Lakes Naval Training Center. A possible theory surfaced suggesting that they were chasing two sailors they met about a month earlier. Their mother heard these rumors and was outraged by these allegations. The police search was intensified and suspects were brought in, turning the case into possibly the greatest missing-persons hunt in Chicago Police history.

Elvis Presley himself made a public statement asking the sisters to return home and relieve their mother's worries. This should have gotten the attention of the girls, since they were big Elvis Presley fans. Still, there was no contact from the sisters.

Finally, the search for the Grimes sisters ended on January 22, 1957 when a construction worker was driving along German Church Road in Burr Ridge. He spotted what appeared to be two unclothed and discarded department store mannequins lying just off the roadway. The "mannequins" turned out to be the nude bodies of the Grimes sisters. The search had now turned into a murder investigation.

The police were said to have questioned about 300,000 people in the case and a good number of these were seriously interrogated. Max Fleig, a 17 year-old boy, became their prime suspect. The police talked him into taking a polygraph test, which he failed. Back then, such a test was considered illegal and since there was no other evidence to prove he did it, the police had to let him go free. Could this have been the killer? It's unlikely we will ever know.

Two other suspects also gave confessions, one being Silas Jane, and the other a man named Benny Bedwell. Silas Jane was a stable owner who was possibly involved in some other murders within the area. Eventually his confession fell apart and he later admitted he had lied to the police. Benny Bedwell's story on the other hand, seemed to make sense and was credible to police investigators.

The police needed to crack the case, so they arrested Benny Bedwell, who worked at an all-night restaurant. Benny told the police he had picked up some underage girls one night in the restaurant. Many people doubted the connection with Benny and the Grimes' but the police went ahead and charged him with murder. These might have been underage girls, but were they the Grimes sisters?

Benny's confession also took the authorities to the scene of the crime, but Benny later told the courts he was shown the spot and coerced into making a confession. Whatever happened there at this point is also a mystery, but he was released from jail and simply disappeared himself. He was never found and his story can still not be proven.

Another attempt to figure out what happened was to find out how the girls had died. The coroner's office listed it as a murder, but an exact cause of death could not be proven. Reports show that the girls had been sexually assaulted, but the information was withheld from the media so that the family could get on with their mourning. The coroner, after the autopsy, could not find a reason of death.

My own research in books and records found that the bodies of the girl's did show some signs of murder. Patricia's abdomen had three ugly wounds, and Barbara's head showed signs of being possibly beaten by some sort of a club. Why are there such conflicting stories in this case?

As to what had happened to the girls still remains a mystery too. There are many theories, including about where they were picked up, and whether it was by some prearrangement and if they were kidnapped. A few believe they ate dinner in the late evening and died shortly after midnight on Dec 28, 1956. If this is true, then why were the bodies found a month later?

There are those that are strongly convinced that they were indeed kidnapped, and were going to be forced into "white slavery" as prostitutes. After they refused, they were then murdered.

Over many years, the case has gotten calls about possible leads, but nothing has since been found. There was a call on the day the bodies were found, saying that they could be found near the racetrack in Tiedtville. The bodies actually were found a very short distance from that location.

Throughout the years there are still many people who are trying to solve this crime. Journalists, police officers, countless detectives, and just your everyday people are searching for that one clue that was possibly missed on the cold January day in 1957. Maybe someday, after over forty-four years since those bodies were found, we will bring this case to a close. Until then, we as a society have learned to remind our children to never talk to strangers, and always be within earshot in case our children yell for some kind of help.

The haunting related to this case involves a portion of German Church Road (83rd Street) that is just east of County Line Road and the section of guardrail on the north side. This is the site where the girl's bodies were dumped. They were found alongside what is known as Devils Creek. There have been numerous reports of a car driving up, what seems to be the sound of something being tossed on the side of the road and the car suddenly driving away and vanishing.

Other reports have claimed to see what appear to be two bodies lying on the side of the road near the guardrail.

The sisters were buried together in Holy Sepulchre Cemetery in Worth, Illinois. They are buried alongside each other in section 37, 21-8. Please respect this grave. No apparent haunting at the gravesite has been reported to this date.

WINCREST NURSING HOME FIRE

It was Friday, January 30, 1976 and a typical cold winter day in Chicago. This seemed like an ordinary day for the many residents and the staff. Around 11:43am smoke was seen coming out of a plywood wardrobe in room 306. The fire alarm rang and the fire department was dispatched immediately.

The building alarm that sounded was either activated by some sort of heat sensor on the third floor or by the fire alarm box near the third floor stairwell. Either of the

two alarms that were activated sent a signal to the fire department to let them know that it was a school, nursing home, hospital, or similar facility where the emergency was occurring. The fire department responds to those alarms by sending additional equipment that consists of two hook and ladder companies, four engine companies, a flying squad, a snorkel, two battalion chiefs, and the division Marshall himself.

The fire department took a little over three minutes to arrive on the scene and verified the fire at 11:46am.

Immediately, the fire personnel entered the building and made their way up to the third floor. Upon arriving here they were met with some heavy smoke and many elderly patients in wheelchairs. There were people choking and gasping for fresh air, some already unconscious. Patients were evacuated as quickly and as safely as the conditions allowed.

At about 12:15pm, the fire department's disaster plan number 3 was placed into effect. This calls for notifying city utilities, other city departments and officials.

The fire was eventually put out by 1:28pm and room 306 was gutted. Patient rooms nearby suffered only minor heat and smoke damage, but this was due to their doors being closed. The first and second floors suffered only minor water damage, and no heat or smoke damage was evident.

The total lives lost were twenty-three, most from smoke inhalation. Total loss to the building was the third floor, room 306, and some minor water damage.

The investigation into the fire eventually brought about a conviction and a man was charged in connection to the blaze. There was a list of recommendations that helped code revisions following the fire. These revisions were immediately made Fire and Building Ordinances of the City:

1) Sprinkler systems in all new and existing nursing homes should be electrically interconnected with the fire

alarm system for water flow. Local valve supervision shall be provided.

2) Formal Fire department emergency training shall be provided to all nursing home personnel every six months to supplement the monthly inspection programs and existing training programs. The nursing home shall provide their staff with emergency training on a monthly basis.

3) Dead-end hallways to be disallowed in all nursing homes.

There were also a number of recommendations to the Board of Health, these included:

1) Training nursing home staff should include:

a) Transporting patients during an emergency

b) The keeping of patients not in immediate danger, calm and comfortable

c) Maintaining areas for family members

d) A "Round-Robin" system of on-call nursing home personnel to be available for emergency duty.

2) Nursing home shall require pre-employment screening as defined by Illinois Department of Public Health Rules and Regulations concerning Long-Term Care Facilities.

3) Disaster plans and drills shall be on file at the Department of Health as well as with the Fire Department. They shall be approved by both departments and posted at all nursing stations.

4) All residents shall have ID bracelets (wristbands) that shall include the name, age, and medical diagnosis.

5) Strict smoking rules within the building. A staff person shall be in constant supervision of these areas assigned.

Though this fire caused very minimal damage to property, many lives were lost. This heavy loss of life was very tragic and with many such events a haunting can follow. Yet as of 2001, as far as we know, this place is not haunted and no reports of any unusual occurrences have been sighted.

FORT DEARBORN

Chekagou, which translates to "wild onion," was actually the original name for the city of Chicago. The city appeared on maps back in 1684, when Tonti and LaSalle passed through this region while traveling to the Mississippi. It would be almost 100 years after they passed before the first settlers arrived.

It was now the year 1779, and a French Canadian trapper and trader by the name of Jean Baptiste Point du Sable established the first trading post. He didn't stay here long and sold off the post in 1800 to another French Canadian named Jean Lalime.

A few years later in 1803, the Americans started pushing west and eventually founded Fort Dearborn. The fort was established on the south bank of what is now the Chicago River. (The place where this fort once stood can be seen on what is now the corner of Michigan and Wacker. It is marked off in the cement near the bridge keeper's house.)

This entire region was isolated from the rest of the country. There was an Indian trail that cut through this territory leading down to Fort Wayne. The soldiers that arrived here to establish the fort had no idea how rough their lives were going to be. They simply found a level piece of land and soon began constructing the fort.

About a year later in 1804, John Kinzie arrived and bought the land from Jean Lalime. He established himself and became the self-appointed civilian leader of the new fort. Soon, Kinzie established good communication with the local Potawatomi Indians, and even began selling and trading them goods. Somehow, Lalime and Kinzie's friendship fell apart and they became bitter enemies. This was possibly due to Kinzie being more successful among the locals. Eventually, their feud escalated into a terrible fight and Kinzie stabbed Lalime to death. Kinzie, who also was wounded, left the fort, but eventually returned. No charges were ever brought up on this incident.

A few months went by, and the outbreak of the War of 1812 brought about the first threat to the fort. Word made its way to the fort that England had taken Mackinac. Orders were soon given to evacuate the fort and hand out any of the fort's leftover supplies to the local Indians.

The handing out of the supplies didn't happen quickly and took what seemed days to begin. Meanwhile, the local Indians started to get restless and encamped outside the fort. Captain Heald, who was in charge, realized he would have to deal with the Indians if they were going to make it to Fort Wayne.

It was now August 12, and Captain Heald held council with the Indians. An agreement was made for exchange of the fort's goods and then they would grant safe conduct for the settlers to Fort Wayne.

All this talk about the surrender of the guns and ammunition didn't go to over well with the soldiers. Instead of turning over the supplies, they decided to dump all the ammunition into a nearby well, and pour out all of the liquor they had left. This made the Indians angry.

Another council was called in the evening. The tribal chiefs agreed to leave the settlers alone but they would have to abandon the fort. Though the officers of the fort disagreed, Captain Heald went ahead and offered to surrender the fort.

Throughout the evening and into the night, the settlers packed up their wagons and passed out any ammunition they could carry. They were going to move out in the morning and make their way to Fort Wayne. Everyone except the sentries that were posted finished packing up and went to bed for that long trip ahead of them.

In the morning, the caravan of wagons, soldiers, civilians, women and children began their trip out of the fort. Soldiers lead the way, followed by the wagons. A portion of Miami warriors followed up the rear. Nobody trusted the Indians and believed the safe conduct passage.

The Potawatomi had provided escort with around 500 Indians. The Indians led them away from the fort and toward a small range of sand hills. Thinking that the Indians would meet up with them around the bend, the contingent from the fort moved on. The Indians placed themselves on a slight elevation while the settlers were closer to the shore.

At about what is now 16th and Indiana Avenue, the scouts suddenly stopped. The Indians turned around and were now charging the settlers. A warning was yelled back down the line but it was not in enough time. Concealed behind the sand ridge were also some Indians who opened fire on the settlers. The soldiers formed a battle line and held off as many of the Indians as they could. After a few minutes though, they were outnumbered and had to give up their horses and wagons.

What had followed after the surrender was plain savagery. Tomahawks were tossed, killing the fort's officers. Mrs. Heald took multiple wounds but was spared her life by a friendly chief. Now after being cut down too less than half the number of settlers that started out on this journey, the garrison surrendered and was promised safe conduct. The death toll was 148 lives lost and of the dead civilians, 86 of them were adults and 12 children.

In this devastating battle, Captain Heald was wounded twice and his wife seven times. She was even going to be scalped but was rescued by Chaudonaire, a St. Joseph Indian who knew her. Chaudonaire had to give up a mule, and bottles of whiskey for her ransom. Captain Heald was not so lucky and was taken prisoner by a local Kankakee Indian. The Indian saw both Captain Heald and his wife in a horrible state and felt pity, so he released them. Chaundonaire and a few others then paddled along the coast and made their way to Mackinac. The British commander there sent the settlers to Detroit and they were exchanged.

John Kinzie and his family managed also to survive. This was possibly because of the friendship they established with the Indians. Kinzie would return to the area about a year later. Things had changed quite a bit and he couldn't get his trading business going again. He soon found himself working for his competitor, the American Fur Company.

The rest of the survivors from the massacre either died soon after or were taken as slaves and sold to the British. The British bought and then released them. The fort was burned down. All the victims remained where they fell and just decayed. It was not until a year later when replacement troops arrived and found the burned down fort and the skeletons.

The settlers then were given a proper burial they deserved. The fort was rebuilt but in 1836 was abandoned since the Chicago settlement was able to fend for itself.

Years ago, the haunting of the old fort was said to involve the troops that were killed by the Indians. This is the area of Wacker and Michigan. The massacre site around 16th and Indiana remained calm until workers there who were repairing the street unearthed some human remains. Carbon dating placed them back in the early 1800's, possibly the victims of the massacre.

Soon after this discovery, people started to see ghostly apparitions fleeing across an open lot on the site. The reports made claimed that people who passed by saw pale figures moving about the area. Some of these figures have been seen running around as in some form of fright. Their mouth is open as if yelling out for help, yet nothing is heard. The apparitions are said to be dressed in early settler clothing, and have been seen around the east side of the present-day intersection. This site is now a parking lot along the railroad tracks, by 16th street.

EASTLAND DISASTER

It was 6:30am and a beautiful summer morning. With the river being calm, the ship floated as if showing off herself with pride. She was moored alongside the south wall of the Clark Street Bridge at Wacker. This was no ordinary ship just floating there either; it was the *Eastland*, the "Speed Queen of the Lakes." She got the name from being the fastest on the Great Lakes, traveling at over 22 knots an hour.

She was beautiful, built of steel, and had ocean-type construction. She stood at four decks high, 269 feet in length and had a 36-foot beam width. This was small, yet its design was made so she could basically glide across the water and navigate the channels. Some reported that this small width would make her top heavy, yet others claimed there wasn't a problem. She passed a federal inspection a few days before, was certified to be sea worthy and the inspectors had even increased her passenger capacity from 2,183 to 2,500.

The crew of the ship started to take on passengers shortly after 6:30am. This was no typical day as the Western Electric Company had sold more than 7,000 tickets to this morning's event. Western Electric Company had chartered the *Theodore Roosevelt*, the *Petoskey*, the *Maywood*, the *Racine*, and the *Rochester*, all who were also being chartered for the picnic and moored near the *Eastland*. With over 7,000 people expected in attendance, no specific ship assignments had been made for the employees. But, because the *Eastland* and the *Theodore Roosevelt* were the newest, most Western Electric employees wanted to be there early to board these ships. And since these two ships were scheduled as the first to depart, there was no doubt that both of the ships would be filled to their capacities.

Now with this being more of a social event for the company, there were many young, teens, and of course, single people in attendance. A lot of these people were actual employees of Western Electric. All were here for a chance to ride these prestigious ships and spend a day on a picnic across the lake in Michigan.

The passengers rushed to get on board the *Eastland*, the crew soon losing count of how many passengers were on board. It was around 6:50am when the ship started to lean. This was possibly due to passengers boarding. The *Eastland's* Chief Engineer ordered the ballast tanks to be filled, trying to compensate for the load. A minute later the ship evened out and everything was again going well.

It was now almost 6:55am and the ship started to lean again to port. Within the next 21 minutes, the ship would be swaying back and forth as crews tried to even the ship out. Passengers thought nothing of this and just were having a grand time. It now was 7:16am and the boat was at a tilt of 15 degrees. The crew once again straightened the ship out, yet water started to come in through openings on the lower port side.

The passengers now were concentrated on what was happening on the port side instead of being spread evenly throughout out the ship. The crew asked many to go over to the starboard side to try and compensate for this 25-30 degree lean. Water at this time was pouring in through the port's lower openings.

To make matters worse, at about 7:28am, a passing Chicago fireboat was going by and blew its whistle to the crowd. This got the attention of most of the passengers, who rushed to see what was going on. Many articles started to fall in the water, chairs, tables, and all different kinds of furnishings from the boat. At 7:30am, the Eastland finally settled over onto its port side in the river.

For many, they were lucky enough to be able to just crawl out and stand on the starboard hull. Many others were either trapped beneath the water, or had been tossed into the river. There were people everywhere and some would later claim that all you could see were people in the water. They were so tightly packed; there was no place for them to tread water if they could.

Immediately, the boats and people nearby started a rescue operation. People dove into the river while others jumped into boats to try and help those in the water. Anything that could float was tossed into the water. Crews were pulling out those who were both dead and alive. Screams of terror were heard from beneath the ship. Those who managed to survive had no way out and drowned. At 8am, all the survivors were reported to have been pulled out of the river.

The ship's hull had to be cut, so that divers could reach those who were trapped inside and under the water. The retrieval of bodies began shortly and then the problem of where to store all the bodies became apparent.

Since no list of passengers was ever started, there was no way to tell who the dead where. The vast amount of bodies had to be identified, but there was no place for this process to take place. The Reid-Murdoch Company, which was just across the river, was used as both a temporary hospital and morgue. Eventually, the coroner suggested they move the dead to the 2nd Regiment Armory located on Washington and Madison.

The 2nd Regiment Armory, by late afternoon, housed some 200 of these bodies. Many families came here to try and identify the dead. Lines of people formed around the block. Some 22 families were entirely wiped out in this disaster. The death toll was finally released and it stood at 835 people. Eventually, all the bodies were claimed.

The *Eastland* disaster has never really been solved. A clear cause could never be reached. Hundreds of lawsuits were eventually filed but most of them were thrown out by the Circuit Court of Appeals. The court made a statement that referred that the owners were not liable for any of the deaths that had happened in the disaster.

The *Eastland* was later sold at public auction in December 1915. The title was later transferred to the government and it was pressed into duty as the gunboat *USS Wilmette*. In 1946, the ship was sold for scrap metal.

The story though goes on. It seems the Clark Street Bridge and the 2nd Regiment Armory refuse to allow this incident to pass through history. There have been reports at the Clark Street Bridge, where screams of terror have been heard. Some even claim to have seen a person's face to break the surface of the water and then disappear. This could be caused by the horrible events being replayed over and over again.

The 2nd Regiment Armory is still in existence, yet it goes by another name. The building today is home to Harpo Studios, the Oprah Winfrey Show. Possible perished passengers who are restless still roam these halls. There have been reports of strange events and encounters, ghostly footsteps, children laughing, and a lady in Gray who is dressed in early 1900 attire. She has been known to be walking the halls. Are all these events related to the *Eastland* disaster?

LASALLE HOTEL

In the heart of Chicago's financial district there once stood an elegant hotel. It rose to over 23 stories tall, made of what many called fireproof material, and was considered the biggest and safest hotel west of New York. This building spared nothing when it came to its interior, as it was the place to be seen. The LaSalle was considered the caterer to the elite. The Illinois Republican Party called this its home for a few years. Even President William Taft used the hotel to conduct business with affairs of state. Though all this seemed wonderful, the building lacked many safety precautions. It could have been compared to any skid row flophouse in the area. It was simply a disaster just waiting to happen.

The disaster did come on June 5, 1946. There were over 1,000 guests registered in 886 rooms within the hotel. Another 100 or so employees were working on the shift. Some of the late night people were still having a good time in the lounge on the ground level. It was the Silver Grill Cocktail Lounge and at around 12:20am, someone here noticed the smell of smoke.

The odor was investigated and was found to be coming out from beneath a panel along the lounge's south wall. A couple of the patrons attempted to put out the fire with the help of some seltzer water and sand. Nobody at the moment even tried to notify the fire department.

This would amount to precious time lost and soon, large sheets of flame were coming out through the paneling and igniting everything in their path. These errors of not notifying the fire department sealed the hotel's fate and possibly lead to the seriousness of the fire.

Since there was no sprinkler system in the building, the fire grew and engulfed the entire lounge area. The fire made its way out of the lounge area and caught anything it could on fire. Some say it moved so fast that the employees had no time to react.

The fire quickly made its way up the opened staircases. Smoke filled the elevator shafts, trapping many people inside the building with no way out. Many people who tried to escape ran into the smoke-filled halls. Disoriented by the smoke, they collapsed.

The fire had been going for about 20 minutes when the fire department received the first call for help. An alarm was transmitted to nearby firehouses. After arriving on the scene, the Battalion Chief decided he had better call in a second alarm and had his driver run to a nearby firebox. Firemen ran hoses and ladders near the building, yet the flames were intense. Ladders were strung and firemen were trying to rescue the occupants of the second and third story windows. A short time later, a 5-11 was called in the office, which sent 61 companies and 300 firefighters to the scene.

Firemen ran hose everywhere and even had a hose cooling off the firefighters in the first floor lobby area. The building's standpipe was hooked up and firemen began to pour water on the upper and penthouse floors. Elevator shafts were being doused with water.

As the lobby area fire was brought under control, the Battalion Chief led some firefighters into the area to search for survivors. All of a sudden, the roof collapsed, trapping the Chief and his men. Nearby firefighters saw this event happen and rushed in to help. They uncovered the Chief, and his 30-man crew, and took all those that needed help to the hospital. The Chief did survive the collapse, but later died at the hospital from smoke inhalation.

At a little over 30 minutes after the collapse the fire in the lobby was brought back under control. This was too late though and by this time, bodies were scattered everywhere. Some of the people were still alive, so the Fire Commissioner called in for personnel and life-saving equipment. With all the rooms to search, the firemen managed to revive over 50 people. Some 1050 people managed to be saved by the firemen in some way.

City Hall, located down the street, was set up as a first-aid station and temporary morgue. There were 42 bodies laid out here in neat rows. Over 200 had received medical attention. There were a total of 61 people who lost their lives in the fire. Fifty of them died at the scene, 9 died upon arrival at the hospital and the remaining two died at the hospital.

An immediate investigation into the fire could find no real problem. The heating and electrical system was in working order. The investigators speculated on a possible cigarette butt being tossed into the elevator shaft. Another report suggested that a light fixture might have been to blame. In either case, nobody was certain how the fire started.

The LaSalle Hotel fire was important because it now placed a value on important things needed in hotels, like an automatic sprinkler system and a fire detection box that was linked to the fire department. An outside fire alarm box and the use of non-flammable material to be used in the hotel lobby area were also mentioned. Also, there were a number of important recommendations that included not using paneling and subdividing all large vertical walls. There were to be fire education classes and drills for all employees. A proposal included labeling all doors in rooms with a map telling guests what to do and where to go in case of a fire. Most importantly, it was recommended that all fire trucks be equipped with two-way radios. There were only three units with radios at the time of the fire in the entire Chicago Fire Department

THE STOCKYARDS

The Union Stockyards once stretched from 39th to 47th, from Ashland to Halsted, in Chicago. They were home to hundreds of cattle pens and home to dozens of buildings. At one time, there were over 100 meatpacking houses here. Built upon a swampland, the local residents referred to this as the "yards."

Many of the workers here were native Europeans. They all lived nearby in their brick and frame buildings. Those that were less fortunate lived in shanties. The air here had the smell of death from daily slaughtering. The leftover waste made its way out via drains and sewers and out into the Chicago River. "Bubbly Creek," as it's often been called, can still be seen around 39th and just west of Racine.

Tragedy struck the "yards" on December 21, 1910. The night watchman, while making his rounds, noticed a fire in the basement in Nelson-Morris Plant No. 7. This was located at Loomis, between 43rd and 44th Streets. After locating the fire's origin, he ran over to building No. 6 to pull the fire alarm. There must have been someone else who saw the smoke too because a second alarm was called into the office. Responding were two firehouses complete with a Battalion Chief and the 2nd Assistant Fire Marshall.

Upon arrival, they found the fire had been traveling up the open staircase doors, possibly left open by the frantic night watchman. The firemen came upon some trouble; since the hydrants were shut down to prevent them from freezing. This took time to get water, since they now had to run to the feeder house to turn on the valve. This massive delay caused the fire to spread even more.

As the fire progressed, a 5-11 alarm was called in, which sent several more fire units and the Chief Fire Marshall to the scene. The commanders all met on the covered loading dock and organized a plan. The Battalion Chief would fight the fire from the north while the Chief Fire Marshall and his assistant fought it on the dock.

The fire seemed to get worse and the water wasn't doing much to control it. All of the sudden, the east wall of the plant blew up from the pressure of the heat; it swung out and dropped on the loading dock. Seeing this entire event happen, the First Assistant Chief sent out the first special alarm. This called out 50 more fire engines, 6 hook and ladders, and numerous special equipment. It also summoned 200 off-duty firemen from the next shift. It took 16 hours to bring the fire under control.

It was now time to dig for the remains of the trapped firemen. They were badly charred and some firemen who were digging dropped from exhaustion. They recovered everyone, including the Fire Marshall himself, who had been crushed by a steel beam.

After it was over, it took 26 hours to put the fire out and recover the dead. One firefighter was carried away in grief by his comrades. He had lost his father and his son, both whom were firefighters. An entire company lost their lives fighting this fire.

The overall property loss was close to $400,000 but the human loss was twenty-one firefighters. This would go down as the darkest day in Chicago Fire Department history, but now stands as the second largest single losses of American Firefighters. It's sad to say that the World Trade Center disaster in September 2001 now ranks number one.

There is a plaque honoring these 21 fallen firemen inside the fire department headquarters at Chicago's City Hall. The cause of the fire was speculated to have been a short in the electrical box, which caused an arc to ignite nearby combustible material. Low water pressure was also a factor in extinguishing the blaze.

These are some of the tragic events that have happened throughout Chicago history. Some of these happened many years ago, while some it seems occurred only yesterday. For most of us, we were not around to witness any of these things. We have just picked up some newspaper or history book and read about them. They touched all our lives in some way or form though, whether it was passed down from the "never talking to strangers" speech from our parents or to that fire drill we practiced at our grade school. Those things were put in place, not for causing some inconvenience, but to provide a safe environment for all of us. This safe environment was not always there years ago and many people lost their lives. To them we should take a moment and pause before we exit beneath that nice lighted sign and remember that it was not always here. Someone lost his or her life so we could safely find our way out of danger.

And that someone may still be lingering behind.

© PHOTO COURTESY OF DALE KACZMAREK

CHICAGO SOUTHSIDE

The southside of Chicago holds many interesting points in historic history that include places like the Jane Adams Hull House, and the Union Stockyards. There were tragic fires, gruesome murders, and even the appearance of the Devil himself. The southsiders may live in a land that many Northsiders would soon choose to forget, but then again Al Capone called the southside his home.

Beverly Unitarian Church - 10244 S. Longwood Drive (Longwood Drive 1832 W., 10200 S.)

Activity - There have been reports of a strange light flickering as if someone was walking window to window with a candle. A lady in a long dress has been reported to

been seen walking the staircase and in the living room area. In 1886, the original owner built this building to resemble an Irish castle he saw while on a trip to Ireland.
FURTHER READING:
Windy City Ghosts, by Dale Kaczmarek (2000)

Firehouse Engine Co.107 - 13th & Oakley (Oakley 2300 W., 1300 S.)

Information - Firefighter Frank Leavy cleaned the windows on the firehouse one day, only to have his handprint reappear later that evening. Legend has it that Frank had told his fellow firefighters that day he had this strange feeling that he was going to die in a fire today. Seconds later after talking to the firefighters the station got a call, where Frank had perished in that fire. The window was accidentally broke by a paperboy in 1944.
FURTHER READING:
Return to the Scene of the Crime, by Richard Lindberg (1999)

Fort Dearborn - 16th Street & Indiana (Indiana 200 E., 1600 S.)

Activity - This was one of many locations along the trail that Indians ambushed settlers. People have reported seeing early settler apparitions near this site, walking and running around in fright. The southside of the bridge area, which is a parking lot, has been the area where these apparitions have been seen. Follow the street around to

the east and you'll be near the historic Prairie District. While there was construction being done on the road near the bridge, workers had recovered bodies that have been carbon dated back to the 1800's.
FURTHER READING:
Haunted Illinois, by Troy Taylor (1999)

Glessner House - 1800 S. Prairie Avenue (Prairie 300 E., 1800 S.)

Activity -Built back in 1886 by John Glessner. There are reports of cold spots around the house, an apparition of man walking on the west side of the building, and a white apparition near the stairs. (Note: This site does give tours on certain days of the week. The oldest home in the city is located a half block down on Prairie. Also Marshall Fields original home is one block south on Prairie Avenue, also numerous other houses. Information is marked on the front gates about the building and past residents.)
FURTHER READING:
Windy City Ghosts, by Dale Kaczmarek (2000)

Hull House - 800 S. Halsted Street. (Halsted 800 W., 800 S.)

Activity - This building is on the current University of Illinois at Chicago campus grounds. Charles Hull had built it in 1856. This was the location of the "devil baby". The child was said to have hooves, horns, and pointed ears. Rumors spread quickly and hundreds came to view

the child, but were only turned away. Residents claimed those were all false allegations about the baby. A guard has been reported sitting at a desk that is no longer there, numerous reports of monk like figures on the stairwell, and a mist on occasion floating by the stairs.
FURTHER READING:
20 years at Hull House, by Jane Adams (1999)

John Hancock (formerly Lourdes) High School - 4034 W. 56th Street (Komensky 4034 W., 5600 S.)

Activity - This was once a private catholic school but it's currently open and in use. Students and faculty are said to hear music and mysterious footsteps throughout the building. No source can be found while being investigated. There have been rumors by students that someone committed suicide in one of the bathrooms, yet no report has ever been found to prove this allegation.
FURTHER READING:
Chicago Haunts, by Ursula Bielski (1998)

St. Turibius - 5646 S. Karlov (Karlov 4100 W., 5600 S.)

Activity - Numerous parishioners have reported a dark apparition by the altar. A former pastor's apparition has been seen between the buildings of the church and rectory, as if exiting one building and then disappearing while entering another. On one occasion while the author was on a Ghost Research Society Excursions into the Unknown Tour the lights on the outside of the church

mysteriously flickered on and off numerous times.
FURTHER READING:
Windy City Ghosts, by Dale Kaczmarek (2000)

Murder Castle - 63rd & Wallace (Wallace 600 W., 6300 S.)

Herman Webster Mudgett, who was a successful businessman, eventually fell into debt and lost this house. Approximately 200 bodies were found in the basement at this location. This house had various secret rooms, an oversize stove and a chute that lead to the basement.

Activity - Though the original building has been torn down, the building is currently a post office. Postal employees report hearing strange sounds and animals walking by do react by pulling away and growl. Also some people walking in or near the building have reported feeling strange vibes, as if something is out of the ordinary.
FURTHER READING:
Windy City Ghosts, by Dale Kaczmarek (2000)

Mount Olivet Cemetery - 2755 W. 111th St. (California 2800 W., 11100 S.)

Activity - Local area residents call this the "Hungry Fence". Numerous car crashes along this fence happened in the 1980's. Research was done, and evidence was found that at a certain precise speed the fence in combination with reflected lighting would cause certain people to have seizures. This would cause them to lose orientation and

crash into the fence. Numerous cemeteries in the area have since then, replaced the fencing with green cyclone fencing, and thus very few accidents have since been reported. This cemetery was also the original gravesite of Al Capone; his grave marker is still in section 52. Catherine O'Leary, the lady whose cow possibly started the Chicago Fire is buried in section 10, northeast corner.
FURTHER READING:
Graveyards of Chicago, by Matt Hucke and Ursula Bielski (1999)

Clarence Darrow Bridge - Jackson Park Lagoon (5800 S., Cornell Dr. 1632 E.)

Activity - An apparition of a nicely dressed man in a camel hair coat is said to be seen walking behind the museum. There have been reports of people trying to yell or talks to the man across the lagoon but only to have witnessed him disappear. People have taken a picture of the lagoon only to find what appears to be a mist or fog hovering above the lagoon.
FURTHER READING:
Haunted Illinois by Troy Taylor (1999)

St. Rita's Church - 6243 S. Fairfield (Fairfield 2733 W., 6200 S.)

Activity - All Soul's Day November 2, 1960, during services, phantom monks frightened and locked in the church parishioners. They were seen in the choir loft and

floating throughout the building.
FURTHER READING:
Windy City Ghosts, by Dale Kaczmarek (2000)
Haunted Illinois, by Troy Taylor (1999)

Kaiser Hall – Archer & Arch (Archer 2900 S., Arch 1316 W.)

Information - This is currently an office and private residential building. Though many years ago, there was a report that the devil himself made an appearance. Local residents refer to this as, "as the day the devil came to Bridgeport." According to legend, the devil appeared as a nicely dressed individual. He picked out the prettiest young lady to dance with. As they danced faster and faster they both disappeared into a puff of flame. Sometime the story is stretched as to a point where all that was left was a pair of hoof marks, which was said to have been burned into the last place the devil touched before they disappeared. (*Windy City Ghosts*, 2000)

Holy Family Church - 1080 W. Roosevelt (Carpenter 1032 W., Roosevelt 1200 S.)

The church survived the Chicago Fire and is the second oldest in the city dating back to 1857. There is a famous ghost story goes back to the 1880's and Father Damen, involving two boys, and their mother. On the altar there are two statues of those boys, watching over and reminding you of that story.

Activity - Parishioners report seeing shadowy figures in the organ loft area. An apparition of an older priest, who passed away, reportedly haunts the main floor of the church.
FURTHER READING:
Windy City Ghosts, By Dale Kaczmarek (2000)

Field Museum of Natural History – 1400 S. Lake Shore Drive (1400 S., Lake Shore Dr. 500 E.)
Information - In 1956, an assistant museum curator whom had been working in the basement complained of being hot and went outside for some fresh air. He chose to lie down in the grass, but moments later he suffered a mild heart attack. The man did survive the heart attack but the grass apparently did not. Even after have being dug up a few feet deep, nothing would grow in that area even after six years. There have been reports of mummies that relocate themselves in the rooms, strange noises being heard, and apparitions of people that seem to appear as if being lost only to disappear after being followed by guards.
FURTHER READING:
Chicago's Street Guide to the Supernatural, by Richard Crowe (2000)

McCarthy House - 35th and Cottage (Cottage 800 E., 3500 S.)
Activity - Elizabeth McCarthy is said to haunt her former home, where she has been seen peering out the

window at the ground below. Her daughters offered to let anyone rent the house for free, but you had to stay out of one room. The room was where Elizabeth would just sit and read in her rocking chair. Nobody took them up on the offer.

FURTHER READING:

Windy City Ghosts, by Dale Kaczmarek (2000)

49th St and Loomis - 4900 S. Loomis (Loomis 1400 W.)

Activity - There have been reports of a headless horseman in this area. The National Guard had set up a command post here during the 1894 railroad riots. Posted here were riflemen and cavalry whom had an encampment nearby. Numerous people were shot down who were protesting the railroads at the time. Many deaths including cavalrymen happened at this location.(Ed. note: I grew up a block away from here and never knew the story until a few years ago, now I understand why us kids hated to walk under the eastside of that bridge after dark. Never actually saw anything, just gave you real uneasy feelings.)

FURTHER READING:

Windy City Ghosts, by Dale Kaczmarek (2000)

Glowing Man of 67th Street - (Western 2400 W., 6700 S.)

Information - A transparent glowing green man was reported to have been seen walking toward a group of reliable people. As the group got closer they both ran off in fright in opposite directions. No other reports have been made since 1965.

FURTHER READING:

Chicago Haunts, by Ursula Bielski (1998)

Visitation Church - 843 W. Garfield Blvd. (Halsted 800 W., Garfield Blvd 5500 S.)

Activity - Monk like figures have been reported on the westside of the church. A former priest was seen at the altar praying. The old rectory at one time was located on the northside of the street across from the church, its now located on the east side of the church.

FURTHER READING:

Haunted Illinois, by Troy Taylor (1999)

Windy City Ghosts, by Dale Kaczmarek (2000)

Lexington Hotel (Al Capone Headquarters) - NE Corner of 22nd and Michigan (Cermak 2200 S., Michigan 100 E.)

Information - This was the site of Al Capone's headquarters back in the 1920's and 1930's. He occupied two floors of this lavish hotel from 1928-1932, rumor has it that it cost over $1500 a day. There are reports that Capone claimed that the ghost of James Clark haunted him. He would have his bodyguard's keep a watchful eye on him at all times, including throughout the night while he slept. There were tunnels under the hotel in which Capone would easily slip in and out of the hotel unnoticed. His original house was located at 7244 S.

Prairie (7200 S., Prairie 300 E.)
FURTHER READING:
Return to the Scene of the Crime, by Richard Lindberg
(1999)

Midway Crash United Flight 533 - 3722 W. 70th Place
(Hamlin 3800 W., 7000 S.)

Information - This is a private residence. On December 8, 1972, a United Airlines pilot was following a missed approach pattern and suddenly crashed into this house. Killed was the owner of the house, her daughter and 43 passengers. Eighteen passengers did manage to survive. Those listed to have died included a U.S. Representative and Mrs. Dorothy Hunt. Mrs. Hunt's husband was indicted in conspiracy to break into the Headquarters of the Democratic National Committee at the Watergate Hotel.
FURTHER READING:
Windy City Ghosts, by Dale Kaczmarek (2000)

Green Hornet Streetcar Collision - State St. and 62nd Place
(State 0 E&W, 6200 S.)

Information - On May 25, 1950 a streetcar rammed into a gasoline tanker truck and caught fire. There were 34 dead and many injuries. The policy back then was to stick to the time schedule no matter what the cost. The bridge they approached was flooded so the train was using an emergency track loop, but traveling at a high rate of speed. By time he saw the tanker truck it was too late.

FURTHER READING:

Return to the Scene of the Crime, by Richard Lindberg (1999)

Stockyard Fire of 1910 - Exchange Av. and Halsted St. (Halsted 800 W., Exchange Av. 4124 S.)

Information - A tragic fire broke out at the Nelson Morris Company's Warehouse No.7, on December 22, 1910. This fire took the lives of 21 firefighters, including the Fire Marshall, a few Captains, Lieutenants, and firefighters. There is an interesting stone gateway at the entrance to the Stockyards. Its one block west of Halsted on Exchange Av. that is worth viewing. The huge empty lot on the NW corner of this intersection is all that remains of the historic International Amphitheater.

FURTHER READING:

Return of the Scene of the Crime, by Richard Lindberg (1999)

Chinatown Area - 211 W. 22nd Place (Wells 200 W., 2200 S.)

Activity - This restaurant seems to be getting some help by a ghost that doesn't mind to help when it's greatly needed. During the peak times when the restaurant is busy, the dirty dishes that seem to pile up mysteriously disappear. Something washes them properly and places them away. No employees claim to have even touched that task, so whoever is doing that

they appreciate the help. Could this building have some sort of poltergeist effect going on?
FURTHER READING:
Windy City Ghosts II, by Dale Kaczmarek (2001)

Ethyl's Party (formerly Tito's) - 2600 S. Wentworth (Wentworth 200 W., 2600 S.)

Activity - This building at one time was a funeral home. Early local residents referred to this as the place where the dead bodies were on display. The television has been known to change channels by itself. A mysterious apparition wearing a trench coat has been seen walking by the bar area. While a band was playing, it seemed to have an extra member on stage for a short period of time. Was this person fulfilling a dream it didn't when the person was alive? Kind of makes you wonder what happens when a funeral home leaves the building, do the temporary residents remain?
FURTHER READING:
Windy City Ghosts II, by Dale Kaczmarek (2001)

The Lincoln Funeral Train - 12th St. Depot (Lake Shore Drive 500 E, Roosevelt 1200)

Information - This historic train that made a trek across numerous states appears to make a number of appearances. One such sighting is just south of the McCormick Place along Lake Shore Drive. The Illinois Central Railroad tracks run parallel along this area and a number of people have observed the Funeral Train. Some say that their watches have stopped and time stands still for those few seconds in history.

FURTHER READING:

Chicago's Street Guide to the Supernatural, by Richard Crowe (2000)

Strange Shape in the Window - 5501 S. Racine (Racine 1200 W., 5500 S.)

Information - This is a private residence. Locals have been doing this for many years hoping to bring justice to those who try to outdo the long arm of the law. A little girl was killed in an automobile accident, an apparent hit-and-run. Her parents chose to dress one of their little girl's dolls in her clothes, and place it in the front window watching for traffic passing by. Could this be a way to get to the conscience of a driver asking to turn themselves in?

FURTHER READING:

Chicago's Street guide to the Supernatural, by Richard Crowe (2000)

DOWNTOWN CHICAGO

The City of Chicago is truly a magnificent city with its roots going back to the great explorers, Marquette and Joliet. A city with a great reputation for its business and politics, yet a city that holds a reputation of being possibly the most haunted in the Midwest. Take your time and look around, while we visit a few of the possible "hot spots" in the downtown Chicago area.

Clark Street Bridge - Between Clark and LaSalle Street Bridges. (Wacker Drive 230 N., Clark Street 100 West)

The Eastland was a steamer ship, which capsized here on July 24, 1915 that killed a total 844 of its 2,500 passengers. A passing ship caught the eyes of many passengers who ran over to one side of the boat causing it to tilt and capsize. Many people were trapped inside the cabins underwater.

Activity - Reports of hearing cries of terror, there is a person's face that appears to be surfacing the water only to disappear. A memorial plague now stands at the corner of the Clark and Wacker, remembering all those who perished in those waters that nice summer day. (See also Harpo Studios, Excalibur, and Bohemian National Cemetery)
FURTHER READING:
Windy City Ghosts II, By Dale Kaczmarek (2001)

Harpo Studios – 1058 W. Washington St. (Aberdeen 1100 W., Washington 100 N.)

The building today is the home of the Oprah Winfrey Show. Yet back during that dreadful day of July 24, 1915, the day of the Eastland disaster, this building housed many bodies of that horrible event. The city had so many bodies at one time that it resorted placing them in buildings that could house bodies on blocks of ice. The building back then was home to the 2nd Regiment Armory.

Activity - Perished passengers are possibly restless in the studio. There are reports of strange events and encounters, ghostly footsteps, children laughing, and a lady in Gray that is dressed in early nineteen hundred attire seen walking the hall. Are these possible events believed to be related to the Eastland disaster?

FURTHER READING:
Windy City Ghosts by Dale Kaczmarek (2000)

Excalibur - 632 N. Dearborn (Ohio 600 N., Dearborn 50 W.)

This building was designed by Henry Ives Cobb in 1896. The building holds reference to two great Chicago area disasters. The first being the Great Chicago Fire, where women went there in hopes of being saved from the fire. There is a report that one man is believed to have jumped from the building to save his own life. The second event, which happened in 1915, was the Eastland disaster. Bodies were possibly stored at this building and at other nearby locations as temporary morgues. The Reid Murdoch Building, 2nd Regiment Armory Building, and a Funeral Home that was on Clark Street are noted many times to be used as those temporary morgues. (Editors note: The author researched this story and could not find any information that this building was used a temporary morgue for that disaster.)

Activity - In the Dome Room, numerous people claimed to see a child playing around the area of the second floor. A child's voice is heard crying in the bathroom. A man in a white tuxedo with red hair, that seems to be glowing, behind a bar that is no longer there. The bar was on the first floor, east side in front of the windows. The women's rest room also on the second floor is reported to be haunted; water faucets turn on by themselves. At times a scent of possibly rotting flesh is reported by the club patrons. Also, candles that mysteriously reignite after being picked up for the night and replaced back on the tables.

FURTHER READING:

Haunted Illinois by Troy Taylor (1999)

Windy City Ghosts by Dale Kaczmarek (2000)

Water Tower – 806 N. Michigan Avenue (Michigan 100 E., Chicago 800 N.)

This is one of the very few buildings that managed to survive the Great Chicago Fire of 1871.

Activity - People walking by often see a ghost of a man peering out the window. While others see a man hanging there with a noose around its neck, there is no record of any man who was hung there. Is this possibly someone who wanted to escape the Great Chicago Fire in the 1800's?

FURTHER READING:

Haunted Places the National Directory by Dennis William Hauck (1996)

Iroquois Theater - 24 W. Randolph (State is 0 E&W, Randolph 150 N.)

This is the current location for the Ford Center for the Performing Arts. On December 30, 1903, a performance of "Mr. Bluebeard" by comedian Eddie Foy was being performed. A fire had broken out causing people to panic, the buildings doors which were designed to swing open caused people in the front to get crushed. The side doors, which had gates, were bolted shut, which made matters worst. Over 603 had perished; some were women and children out of school for the holidays. Forty of those that perished were schoolteachers for the City of Chicago. The tight ropewalker was the only performer who died, among 500 personnel. Chicago Fire Department extinguished the blaze within about a half hour. Fire precautions were in effect but not closely followed.

Activity - The alley behind the theater is often referred to as "Death Alley". Firefighters stacked numerous bodies in that alley, while others had jumped and some had even fallen to their death to escape the fire.
FURTHER READING:
The Great Chicago Theater Disaster, by Marshall Everett (1904)
Windy City Ghosts by Dale Kaczmarek (2000)

John Hancock Building - 875 N. Michigan (Michigan 100 E., Delaware 900 N.)

Captain George Wellington Streeter had cursed this land back in 1921 when he died. He claimed that the land was not part of Chicago, and took up refuge there, claiming squatter's rights. The city tried many times to evict him off this land, but Captain Streeter was a great with a rifle, and could easily defend his land. Numerous attempts were made to remove him including trying to get him for tax evasion. There was one incident where a man was shot and killed, Captain Streeter was charged and convicted of murder.

Activity - There was one reported death during the construction of the building. Also a lady by the name of Laurie Kowalski plunged naked from the top of the building. Police were baffled on how a person could plunge through double pane glass, which needs a force of 300 lbs. to break. The First Church of Satan, founded by Anton Levey was also born and raised here.

FURTHER READING:

Chicago Haunts, by Ursula Bielski (1998)

Windy City Ghosts by Dale Kaczmarek (2000)

O'Leary Barn - 558 W. DeKoven Street (DeKoven 1100 S., Jefferson 600 W.)

Information - This is the site where the O'Leary barn was located. Urban legend has it that the O'Leary cow kicked over a lantern, which ignited hay and other material. The 1871 fire caused as much damage to property as $191,000,000, about 300 people died, and over 100,000 people left homeless. Was it the O'Leary cow or Daniel "Peg Leg" Sullivan, who started the fire? The O'Leary home did mange to survive the fire, but not the cow and barn. The street addresses were renumbered in this area after the fire, this site was known before as 137 DeKoven. (See also Mt. Olivet Cemetery)

FURTHER READING:

Great Chicago Fires, by David Cowan (2001)

Peter Schuttler Mansion - Northeast Corner of Aberdeen and Adams (Aberdeen 1100 W., Adams 200 S.)

Activity - The building was on the northeast corner, now an abandoned warehouse. Strange noises and animals tend to react to the property. This was the site of possibly the grandest house in the City of Chicago. Schuttler had stubbed his toe and died of blood poisoning. He cursed the entire property on his deathbed. His widow reportedly committed suicide one night when his ghost appeared. Could this possible haunting be the reason why this warehouse becomes vacant so quick?
FURTHER READING:
Windy City Ghosts by Dale Kaczmarek (2000)

Rubloff Building - 680 N. Lake Shore Drive (Ohio 600 N., Lake Shore Drive 500 E.)

Information - Certain sections of this building is for private residences, mainly the upper floors. This building's address was once 666; it was changed after numerous complaints from tenants. Seems like they did not want to have an address such as that, and be known that they live with possibly the devil. There have been a few reports that the east lobby area is possibly haunted. Some hear a muffled female's voice, and others have claimed to see a lady dressed in early nineteen hundred attire that seems to be only to wandering around and disappears within a few seconds later.
FURTHER READING:
Chicago's Street Guide to the Supernatural by Richard Crowe

Haymarket Riots - Randolph St. between Halsted and DesPlaines Ave. (Randolph 150 N., Halsted 800 W., DesPlaines 640 W.)

Information - On Tuesday May 4, 1886 this was the site where union workers rallied to protest strike breakers and protest the police tactics that have been used against previous strikers. Numerous men were reported killed, including a police officer, while dozens were injured. The protest was for higher wages for an eight hour day and better working conditions.

FURTHER READING:
Return to the Scene of the Crime, by Richard Lindberg (1999)
Chicago Municipal Reference Library, City of Chicago

Chicago Transit Authority El Train Wreck - Wabash and Lake St. (Wabash 50 E., Lake St. 200 N.)

Information - This is the site of that icy cold day on Feb.4th 1977 that a train traveling 10mph had collided with another waiting El Train stopped on a curve. The wreck had caused 11 deaths, yet over 1,000 rush hour passengers were boarded on both trains. The CTA has not had any other incidents since this dreadful accident.

FURTHER READING:
Return to the Scene of the Crime, by Richard Lindberg (1999)

Hooters Restaurant 660 N. Wells (Ontario 640 N., Wells 200 W.)

Activity- There seems to be activity throughout the building. Ghostly footsteps are heard, and phantom

voices that seem to be calling your name. Some of these events have taken place in the basement area, while others at no apparent spot in the building. Waitresses have felt somebody placing a hand on their shoulder, yet they turn around and nobody is there. Could these events be related to the Great Chicago Fire?
FURTHER READING:
Windy City Ghosts II, by Dale Kaczmarek (2001)

Billy Goat Tavern - 430 N. Michigan (Illinois Ave. 500 N., Michigan 100 E.)

Information - Back in 1945 a curse was placed on the Chicago Cubs while they played Detroit. It seems the Cubs got tired of letting the goat in even though he did have a ticket of its own. Well after the ushers refused to let the patrons in, they walked away with something else on their mind. Even up until this date, that curse has still not been lifted. Numerous attempts have been made in the recent years to allow the goat entry, but still the curse remains intact. Could this be a lesson to be well learned to be kind to animals?
FURTHER READING:
Windy City Ghosts II, by Dale Kaczmarek (2001)

The Red Light Restaurant - 820 W. Randolph (Halsted 800 W., Randolph 150 N.)

Activity - This modern day restaurant seems to have a resident ghost that likes to have a little fun on its own. People have reported that they hear their name being called, only to turn around and nobody is there. Doors have known to lock, while nobody on the premises at the time has keys to unlock them. Lights have been known to dim by themselves. Could this be a ghost just out to set the romantic mood by dimming the lights or saving electricity?

FURTHER READING:

Windy City Ghosts II, by Dale Kaczmarek (2001)

CHICAGO'S NORTHSIDE

The northside of Chicago is the final resting place of many notable Chicagoans. This is part of the city where numerous mishaps including massacres to ruthless gangster killings have taken place. From one of the FBI'S largest manhunts in Chicago to the mysterious Totem pole. Let's take you back to yesteryear where Capone and Moran fought over sections of the city.

St. Valentines Day Massacre - 2122 N. Clark (Dickens 2100 N., Clark 300 W.)

Activity - This is the site where back in 1929; Al Capone killed seven members of the "Bugs" Moran Gang. Posing as police officers, Capone's men entered the garage, attempted to shake down the men but only in a bath of bullets. Though the building is actually gone and a nursing home is currently built a little to the north here, there are reports of strange sounds being heard and animals either refuse to walk by or strangely react. The place where the wall once stood is in the area of the five trees south of the nursing home. Some say this could be the event being replayed on that bloody day of Feb 14th 1929, St. Valentines Day. Rumors have been told that the bricks that were scavenged from the old building bring bad luck to the current owners.

FURTHER READING:
Return to the Scene of the Crime, by Richard Lindberg (1999)

Biograph Theater - 2433 N. Lincoln Avenue (Fullerton 2400 N., Dayton 825 W.)

This theater is currently open and shows recent releases. Though in 1934 in a hail of gunfire, the FBI ruthlessly shot and killed a man they identified as John Dillinger. So many people claim it was not Dillinger they had shot, but the FBI stands by the story that Dillinger had plastic surgery.

Activity - The apparition of a man has been seen by many people running out the theater and into the alley next door. Some claim it is the ghost of John Dillinger, while other say it is the ghost of Jimmy Lawrence a small-time hood, whom the FBI accidentally shot on that day.

Did Dillinger double-cross the FBI and remain free? Was he that careless to fall into a trap?
FURTHER READING:
Return to the Scene of the Crime, Richard Lindberg (1999)

Red Lion Pub -2446 N. Lincoln Avenue (Fullerton 2400 N., Altgeld 2500 N.)

This 1862 building has gone from a three-story apartment into a prospering English pub. The owner John Cordwell many years ago had installed a memorial, complete with stained glass and a brass plaque in the name of his father, whom was buried in England without a tombstone.

Activity - Many people have reported feeling dizzy when they walked past the window. A twenty-year-old retarded girl who died in the building might be associated with the strong smell of lavender. Also the women's restroom on the second floor has had some type of energy that traps the patrons inside. Numerous other ghosts have also been reported in the building, including a man that is seen walking up the stairs, a woman in dressed in some sort of 1920's outfit, and also a man wearing some type of a black hat. Can this be some sort of portal, or just previous patrons paying tribute to the place they enjoyed?
FURTHER READING:
Haunted Places the National Directory, by Dennis William Hauck (1996)

St. Andrew's Pub -5938 N. Broadway (Thorndale 5934 N., Broadway 600 W.)

Activity - A previous owner by the name of Frank Giff died from falling off a bar stool in the tavern. Customers and employees report cold spots throughout numerous areas of the building. There are reports of ashtrays, glasses and other objects being moved in the bar without any human power.

FURTHER READING:

Haunted Places the National Directory, by Dennis William Hauck (1996)

That Steak Joynt (formerly at) - 1610 N. Wells (North Av. 1600 N., Wells 200 W.)

Activity - There have been apparitions reported to be seen in this former building. People have heard of strange sounds, some have been touched by someone or thing that in not visible, and phantom footsteps.

FURTHER READING:

Windy City Ghosts, by Dale Kaczmarek (2000)

Victorian House Antiques (formerly at) - 806 W. Belmont (Halsted 800 W., Belmont 3200 N.)

Activity - This house was an antique shop that dates back to the year 1879. In the 1880's a women was murdered in the house, followed later by four people dying in the attic from a fire. There are numerous cold spots throughout the building. People have witnessed cabinets and doors opening and closing without human intervention.

FURTHER READING:

Chicago Street Guide to the Supernatural, by Richard Crowe (2000)

Kwa Ma Rolas Totem Pole - Lake Shore Dive and Recreation Drive (Lake Shore Dr. 500 E., Recreation Dr. 3600 N.)

Activity - This is an authentic Indian Totem Pole that was donated. Numerous reports of the figures changing position, people have taken a picture one day and coming back to find that the figures are in the wrong order. Various local newspapers have had pictures sent to them showing this phenomenon.

FURTHER READING:

Windy City Ghosts, by Dale Kaczmarek (2000)

Calvary Cemetery - 301 W. Chicago Avenue (Juneway Terr. 7736 N., Sheridan Rd. 400 W.)

This cemetery dates back to 1859; it borders Chicago and the suburb of Evanston. Pick up a map at the office. A few monuments worth seeing are "Artie and Willie" (eastside of section Q). Famous Chicagoans buried here include Charles Comiskey (section M). Former Chicago Mayor John Kelly (section I), John M. Smyth (section N), and Edward Hines the lumber king (section M, is a few steps right off Sheridan Road on the southside of the road).

Activity - Locals have nicknamed him "Seaweed Charlie," whom has been observed on numerous occasions crawling across Lake Shore Drive. The apparition covered in seaweed seems to be crawling across Lake Shore Drive as if exiting from the Lake Michigan waters. He seems as if he is trying to gain entry into the cemetery. Could this be one of those numerous training pilots from the World War?

FURTHER READING:

Graveyards of Chicago, by Ursula Bielski and Matt Hucke (1999)

Bohemian National Cemetery - 5225 N. Pulaski (Bryn Mawr 5600 N., Pulaski 4000 W.)

This cemetery dates back to the 1870's. Pick up a map at the office. Famous Chicagoans buried here include former Mayor Anton Cermak (SW corner of section 21), and many Western Electric Employees whom were victims of the Eastland Disaster (section 16). The chapel and civil war area are a good area to view.

Activity - There have been reports of a black early model phantom car and people dressed in attire from possibly the 1920's sighted in the cemetery. The sightings have been in numerous times of the day. There have been many unexplainable accidents along Bryn Mawr Avenue, possibly because of the fencing.

FURTHER READING:
Graveyards of Chicago, by Ursula Bielski and Matt Hucke (1999)

Robinson Woods - East River road at Lawrence Avenue. (Lawrence 4800 N., East River Rd. 8800 W.)

In 1829 the Robinson's were granted land here for the saving the lives of a white family during the Fort Dearborn Massacre. The legend in this area claims that eventually the Robinsons were killed hereby jealous tribal members.

Activity - There have been reports of strange faces appearing from behind the foliage, strange noises being heard include tom-toms and woodcutting. People passing through the area have reported seeing strange lights moving through the woods. Photos of the area show unexplainable lights.

FURTHER READING:
Chicago Haunts, by Ursula Bielski (1998)

Graceland Cemetery - 4001 N. Clark (Irving Park Rd. 4000 N., Southport 1400 W.)

The cemetery had its first burials in 1865. Pick up a map at the office, there are not sections marked off. Famous Chicagoans that are buried here including: Marshal Field, Cyrus H. McCormick, George M. Pullman, Allan Pinkerton, John Glessner, Daniel Burnham, William

W. Kimball, just to name a few. Numerous millionaires are buried by the lake in the northeast area.

Activity - The Dexter Graves monument is rather unique; it's often called the "statue of death." It resembles a hooded figure with only a small portion of its face exposed. Local legend has it that you can never take a picture of this gravesite. There is also a life size statue of a young girl holding a parasol marks the grave of Inez Clarke. The statue is supposed to disappear on numerous occasions only to reappear later when you return to check on it. On the anniversary of her death sobbing is heard and the statue is said to be crying tears. Another interesting place is the underground vault of Ludwig Wolff, which is to be haunted by a green-eyed canine that howls at the moon.

FURTHER READING:

Graveyards of Chicago, by Matt Hucke and Ursula Bielski (1999)

Our Lady of Angels - 909 N. Avers (Chestnut 900 N., Avers 3834 W.)

Information - On December 1, 1958 a fire started in a trash drum in the basement stairwell of the school. The first fire engine on the scene arrived twenty minutes after the fire had possibly started. It was first misdirected to the church around the corner. Many nuns and children were trapped, some even jumping out the window to the ground two stories below. It was all over within 45 minutes, overall ninety children, and three nuns died on that day. Yet one hundred sixty children were saved.

In 1959, chapter 78 of the municipal code of Chicago was amended to include schools for fire protection devices.

(See also Suburbs Section, Queen of Heaven Cemetery)
FURTHER READING:
To Sleep with the Angels, By David Cowan and John Kuenster (1996)
Great Chicago Fires, by David Cowan (2001)

Rosehill Cemetery - 5800 N. Ravenswood Ave. (Ardmore 5800 N., Western Av. 2400 W.)

This is the largest and oldest cemetery in Chicago, dating back to 1859. It holds the remains of over 200,000 individuals. There are a lot of good things here to view, including the huge mausoleum. Famous Chicagoans buried in that mausoleum include John G. Shedd (far NE side), Richard W. Sears (located to the right of the stairs going up), and Aaron Montgomery Ward (far NE, not to far from Shedd). All three of these men are buried very close to each other in the NE section on the first floor of the mausoleum.

Activity - The nicely dressed apparition of Richard Warren Sears has been seen wandering the area around his tomb. Could he possibly be trying to meet with his competitor Aaron Montgomery Ward? Also, moaning and chains rattling are heard at the crypt of Charles

Hopkinson (located outside in section D) a real estate tycoon who became rich during the Civil War. A groundskeeper in 1995 saw what looked like a lady standing or rather floating by a tree, only soon to have seen her melt away. The following morning the administration received a call from a woman who reported her deceased aunt made an unexpected visit to her the night before. The aunt was buried without a burial marker and was not remembered.

FURTHER READING:
The Civil War at Rosehill, by David Wendell (1990)

Marge's Pub - 1758 N. Sedgwick St. (North Av. 1600 N., Sedgwick 400 W.)

Activity - There is possibly poltergeist activity or a very playful ghost at this location. Numerous events that include, flying and disappearing objects, mysterious fires, or objects moving in order to attract some sort of attention. A bunch of shot glasses were to have flew off the bar without any type of human intervention. A regular male patron, whom recently died, didn't get along to well with a regular female patron. One day she suddenly became a victim of an apparent mishap. While she reportedly did not stop from bad mouthing him after his death and she chose to sit in his regular chair. Moments later she flew off the chair into some tables, leaving her shoes still at the edge of the bar. Was this possibly the male's mischievous ghost getting revenge?

FURTHER READING:
Haunted Places the National Directory, by Dennis William Hauck (1996)

Adolph Luetgert House - SW corner Diversey and Hermitage (Diversey 2800 N., Hermitage 1734 W.)

Adolph Luetgert wanted to be known as the "Sausage King of the World." He married Louisa Bicknese, who was 10 years younger than him. She mysteriously disappeared one night after numerous family quarrels. Detectives found a wedding band with the initials "L.L.," and a small bone in a vat in the sausage factory. They eventually charged him with murder of his wife, though no body was ever recovered.

Activity - After her death, a white-clad woman was seen in the old house and also in the old sausage factory. Though both of those buildings have been gone for numerous years, legend has it she reappears on the anniversary of her death. Is this the possible ghost of Louisa Luetgert?

FURTHER READING:
Windy City Ghosts, by Dale Kaczmarek (2000)

Wincrest Nursing Home Fire - 6326 N. Winthrop (Devon 6400 N, Winthrop 1100 W.)

Information - A fire had started in the building on January 30, 1976. The nursing home was a very modern and very well operated. The problem arose when the personnel tried to put the fire out by themselves causing significant delay in evacuation time. Very little smoke and water damage was reported, though a total of 23 people had perished. The investigation into this fire had set yet another standard in fire codes for the City of Chicago, and a person was eventually charged in connection with the fire.

FURTHER READING:

Chicago's Street Guide to the Supernatural, by Richard Crowe (2000)

The Bucktown Pub - 1658 W. Cortland St. (Ashland 1600 W., Cortland 1900 N.)

Activity - This apparent ghost that haunts this location like to have a little fun with the new bartenders. Numerous bar supplies, ranging from napkins to glasses have been known to tossed across the room. The jukebox turns itself on at times, maybe to liven up the atmosphere. Could this be an old owner or bartender just out to give the new help some mischief?

FURTHER READING:

Windy City Ghosts II, by Dale Kaczmarek (2001)

Acacia Park Cemetery - 7800 W. Irving Park Rd. (Harlem 7200 W., Irving Park Rd. 4000 N.)

Activity - This was the Captain of the "Christmas Ship," which every year docked at the Clark Street Bridge in downtown Chicago. His name, Captain Herman

Scheuenemann of the schooner Rouse Simmons, perished in the waters of Lake Michigan on November 23, 1912. The ship would make a trip to Michigan to bring back fresh cut affordable tress so that everyone could afford one. At times Captain Scheuenemann would give the trees away to the needy. Strangely though, his wife's grave is said to produce the scent of fresh cut spruce and balsam. Her grave is in section called Westaria, 21-4.
FURTHER READING:
Graveyards of Chicago, by Ursula Bielski and Matt Hucke (1999)

O' Hare Hilton - O'Hare Airport Located across from Terminal 2
        Activity - In one of the rooms, many years ago a man hung himself in an apparent suicide. The room has had cold and warm spots reported. Customers have always asked the front desk for another room because of all the noise in the room and temperature that changed constantly. The hotel has been sound proofed and should not have any loud noises from the jet engines heard within the building. Though the room is actually situated next to an elevator bank, it should not produce enough noise to keep a customer awake. Could this have been some cry for help back on the night of the suicide?
FURTHER READING:
Windy City Ghosts II, by Dale Kaczmarek (2001)

CHICAGO SUBURBS

The many surrounding suburbs of Chicago hold many interesting tales of tragic events and hauntings. There have been hitchhiking apparitions, mysterious balls of lights, phantom animals, and disappearing houses. Bodies have been dumped within cemeteries; ghostly figures have been seen exiting cemeteries. Unusual events seem to plague certain areas, yet certain areas that have no apparent reason to be haunted. Is there some sort of power that draws people to it? We'll look at some of these areas and you'll be the judge to decide.

FOREST PARK

Jewish Waldheim Cemetery - 1800 S. Harlem (Harlem 7200 W, 1800 S.)

Activity - A woman's ghost dressed in 1920's attire has been reported to be hitchhiking along the road near this cemetery. She then only disappears near the cemetery gates, where an old house once stood.

FURTHER READING:

Chicago Haunts, by Ursula Bielski (1998)

Woodlawn Cemetery - 7600 W. Cermak Rd. (Cermak Rd. 2200 S., Harlem 7200 W.)

This is the site of Showmen's Rest, and also the final resting place for the performers from the Great Circus Train Wreck of 1918. The section is on the southside of the cemetery along the Cermak street side. There are five elephant statues that mark the section, including a nice size memorial stone.

Activity - Sounds of elephants crying in the distance are often heard. Walk around and read some of the grave markers in this section.

FURTHER READING:

Graveyards of Chicago, by Ursula Beilski and Matt Hucke (1999)

NORTH RIVERSIDE

Frank Nitti's Suicide - Cermak Road 1 block west of Harlem (Cermak Rd. 2200 S., Harlem 7200 W., just west of

Harlem near the Toys R Us)

Activity - Frank Nitto or Nitti depending on the story you hear, committed suicide at the site on these railroad tracks back on March 19, 1943. People have seen an apparition of a man walking down these tracks, only to have then disappeared. (See Mt. Carmel Cemetery)
FURTHER READING:
Windy City Ghosts II, by Dale Kaczmarek (2001)

Village Commons - 2401 S. DesPlaines Ave. (DesPlaines 8000 W., 2400 S.)

Information - This is the site of the old Melody Mill Ballroom. There have been reports of a 1920's Big Band still heard being played throughout the day. The sounds are often heard when the buildings recreation activities are going on.
FURTHER READING:
Chicago's Street Guide to the Supernatural, by Richard Crowe (2000)

RIVERSIDE

Stop Sign - Intersection of Riverside Rd. and Olmsted (Riverside Rd. 7700 W., Olmsted 3700 W.)

Information - Along Riverside Road there are intersections and trees that one need pay close attention to. The road snakes around numerous trees and you need to watch your speed. The stop sign at this location has been known to be dripping blood on more than one occasion. Could this be nature's way of reminding us to

slow down through this curvy road along the river?
FURTHER READING:
Windy City Ghosts II, by Dale Kaczmarek (2001)

BROOKFIELD
Alonzi's Villa - 8828 Brookfield Rd. (Brookfield Rd. 3700 S., 8800 W.)

Information - This building has two ghosts that roam the property. The apparitions of a little girl and her dog have been seen playing throughout the building. At times there is the sound of voices and people bowling. Could this be the events of the old bowling alley that once stood here? Are the little girl and her dog keeping themselves occupied while her parents bowled many years ago? (Ed. note, this building is no longer there.)
FURTHER READING:
Windy City Ghosts II, by Dale Kaczmarek (2001)

CICERO
Morton College - 3801 S. Central (Pershing Rd. 3900 S. Central Av. 5600 W.)

Activity - Strange sounds of footsteps and a mysterious cloud like apparition is often seen roaming the halls and classrooms. There has been no apparent reason connected to the current college for this type of event to be happening here. The land the college was built upon was a marshland. It was back then that and a man's body was found. Also a missing 18 year-old freshman could be possibly linked here.

FURTHER READING:
Haunted Places the National Directory, by Dennis William
Hauck (1996)
Windy City Ghosts, by Dale Kaczmarek (2000)

St. George's Orthodox Church - 1220 South 60th Court
(Roosevelt Rd 1200 S., 60th Crt. is one block west of
Austin 6000 W.)

Activity - The statue of the Virgin Mary began
weeping tears here back in 1994. A similar event took
place at St. John's Church on 52nd Throop in Chicago.
Both events were inspected and reported to be miracles.
FURTHER READING:
Chicago's Street Guide to the Supernatural, By Richard
Crowe (2000)

CLARENDON HILLS
Country House Restaurant - 241 W. 55th Street (West of Rt.
83, 4 blocks)

Activity - A woman's apparition has been reported
to be seen throughout the restaurant. The woman has
been known to try to lure men up to a former upstairs
bedroom. Loud mysterious noises are heard, doors
opening and closing by themselves, and even a baby
crying. Could this be a former employee or patron?
FURTHER READING:
Windy City Ghosts, by Dale Kaczmarek (2000)

BERWYN

Moline House - 3101 Wesley Avenue (Wesley 6700 W., 3100 S.)

Activity - This is a now a private residence. There have been reports of a man in overalls who seems to be carrying a pitchfork. A woman=s voice has been heard whispering. The doors have been known to open and close, including locking by themselves. Family pets seem too been locked in the basement, when no one apparently placed them there.

FURTHER READING:

Haunted Illinois, by Troy Taylor (2001)

Windy City Ghosts, by Dale Kaczmarek (2000)

HILLSIDE

Mt. Carmel Cemetery - 1100 S. Wolf Road (Roosevelt Rd 1200 S., Wolf Rd. 11200 W.)

There are many people buried here that are worth stopping to visit. Pick up a map across the street at the Queen of Heaven cemetery Office. The graves of Al Capone (section 35 near the Greco grave marker), Frank Nitti (section 32), Julia Buccola Petta (section A directly across from the cemetery office), Dion Deany O' Banion (section L, grave is marked with a white huge obelisk) and Earl Hymie Weiss (section K, it's a private mausoleum)

Activity - Legend has the Al Capone haunts his own grave to protect it from those who try vandalize it. The ghost of Julia "the Italian Bride" Buccola Petta is said to

roam along the north part of the cemetery along Harrison.
FURTHER READING:
Graveyards of Chicago, by Ursula Bielski and Matt Hucke
(1999)

Queen of Heaven Cemetery - 1200 S. Wolf Road
(Roosevelt Rd 1200 S., Wolf Rd. 11200 W.)

Information - Pick up a map at the office for this cemetery, and for Mt. Carmel cemetery located across the street. They both share the same office. There are two events that can be related to this cemetery. The first back in 1958 the Our Lady of Angels Fire, the memorial can be found in the west corner of section 18. Twenty-five of the victims were buried here in a mass grave. People who visited here reported a smell of smoke, felt the pain suffered by the victims, and also a burning sensation felt in their nose. There were also many visions of the Blessed Mother seen here in 1990 through 1992. There is a huge cross that marks the location, it can be found across from section 12 along Wolf Road. This is the site where many have traveled to try to be cured or have seen the apparent vision. (See also Tragic Events)
FURTHER READING:
Graveyards of Chicago, by Matt Hucke and Ursula Bielski
(1999)

STICKNEY

Mt. Auburn Cemetery - 4101 S. Oak Park Avenue (Pershing Rd. 3900 S., Oak Park Av. 6800 W.)

Activity - There have been reports of a woman's apparition and house that disappears within the cemetery. The woman's ghost has been spotted on the west side of the cemetery, while the house in many locations throughout the cemetery.

FURTHER READING:

Windy City Ghosts II, by Dale Kaczmarek (2001)

JOLIET

Rialto Theater -15 E. Van Buren St.(Located in Joliet's City Center, it's three blocks east of the river, south of Route 30, and 3 blocks west of 171. 815-726-7171)

Activity - A strange glowing light appears around the piano, it looks like a figure of a female. Cleaning people have reported pulling out chairs to sweep, then coming back into the room to only find they have been replaced. Handprints reappear on mirrors minutes after they have been cleaned. Also the chairs in the theater manage to move to various positions by themselves. Lights have been known to flicker on by themselves.

FURTHER READING:

Chicago's Street Guide to the Supernatural, by Richard Crowe (2000)

JUSTICE

Resurrection Cemetery - 7200 S. Archer Road (7900 S., Roberts Rd. 8000 W.)

Southside of Chicago's most famous ghost has been seen here many times. There have been reports that a blond haired girl has been haunting this cemetery since 1939. Local legend has it Mary Bregovy or "Resurrection Mary" as many local residents like to call her, was killed in a car accident after attending a dance at the O'Henry Ballroom (now the Willowbrook Ballroom). She has been reported to have been buried in section MM plot 9819. Good luck on finding that grave, it doesn't seem to exist. Other records have indicated that a possible Mary Rozanc, or Mary Bregovy might be "Resurrection Mary". Again no record or grave could be found.

Activity - There have been many occasions that a faceless woman has been seen walking, or hitchhiking along Archer Avenue. In 1976, she was spotted holding the bars of the entrance, as though trying to get out of the cemetery one night, her hand prints were etched in the metal bars. Those bars are located on the exiting side of the cemetery entrance. The cemetery denies the happening, and the bars were removed and repainted, only to have those handprints reappear. She has been known to appear in front of passing motorists when at the last second she vanishes. Motorists claim to have hit a young woman only to stop a few feet later and get out to find there is nobody there. Also, the mausoleum lights have been known to go on by themselves when that building has been closed and nobody is working. There have been sightings of hooded like monks on the 79th street side, also including glowing balls of lights. Take note that a deer population lives within the cemetery and is often spotted at dusk.

FURTHER READING:
Haunted Illinois, Troy Taylor (1999)
Windy City Ghosts, by Dale Kaczmarek (2000)
Chicago Haunts, by Ursula Bielski (1998)

Bethania Cemetery - 7701 S. Archer Road (7900 S., 8700 W.)

Activity - The cemetery opened back in 1894. This has been the site for satanic worship, and a caretaker's ghost. The apparition has been known to be raking and burning leaves just inside the cemetery fence along the 79th street side. This strange encounter is often reported after the midnight hour. Also a report of a bloody apparition running across the street from the apartment area on the Kean Avenue side then vanishes. Drivers have been temporary blinded by a shiny object in the hand of the apparition when encountered.

FURTHER READING:
Windy City Ghosts, by Dale Kaczmarek (2000)

The Why Not Drive In – 7930 Frontage Road (7800 S., Archer crosses at 8700 W., just west of the Justice Police Station on the Frontage Road)

Information - This site is rumored to be haunted by a female apparition who drives a 1965 convertible. She has been known to ask men to follow her, when they do she seems to be driving further and further from them. Eventually she disappears in what seems like a fog or mist, after the men exit that hazard in the road, there is no sight of the convertible. This seems to be one of those females leaving the men in the dust or shall we say fog.
FURTHER READING:
Windy City Ghosts, by Dale Kaczmarek (2000)

LEMONT

St. James Cal Sag – 106th & Archer Road (This is just a 2-3 mile drive off I-55 on Rt. 83 South)

This location has existed since 1834. It has been noted that this is the land that seems to breathing. Locals refer to this location as "Monks Castle".

Activity - This area is patrolled by police heavily. Reports of ghost like monks exiting the woods and walking up the hill that only seem to have disappeared. A phantom horse and carriage have been reported to ride up toward the church where a female gets in and the carriage heads back down to only disappear at the gates.
FURTHER READING:
Lemont Centennial, copyright (1973)
Graveyards of Chicago, by Ursula Bielski and Matt Hucke (1999)

MIDLOTHIAN

Bachelors Grove - 143rd Just East of Ridgeland (14300 S., Ridgeland 6400 W., you'll see a communication tower on the southside of the street, park in the parking lot on the north side of street. Walk across the street and into the roped off area for a few hundred feet.)

Information - Police patrol this area heavily. The woods do close at sunset, and they will tow your vehicle and arrest you. This is possibly the most haunted location in the Midwest and probably America. This cemetery was abandoned many years ago. It was used during the building of the Cal Sag Channel, where many men mostly bachelors died during construction. The cemetery is located about a quarter mile south directly across from the Rubio Woods. The entrance is the blocked access road, next to the communication tower; you may only walk into this area. Again, park you car across the street and walk in.

Activity - Numerous sightings of ghost like figures, animals, a disappearing house, and strange mysterious lights. The pond is haunted by a farmer that seems to be plowing the area with a horse. Some people report seeing a black and tan rottweiler protecting the trail to the cemetery, yet the dog doesn't bark but just watches what you are doing. A few seconds later when the turn to look at the dog it had suddenly disappeared. Could this be a phantom dog?

FURTHER READING:
Psychic City Chicago, by Brad Steiger (1976)
Windy City Ghosts, by Dale Kaczmarek (2000)

Midlothian Turnpike - 143rd Just East of Ridgeland (Ridgeland 6400 W., 14300 S.)

Activity - There are strange phantom cars that suddenly appear and collide with vehicles only to have then disappeared. The events sound as if you were in a car accident only to find nothing had actually happened.
FURTHER READING:
Windy City Ghosts, by Dale Kaczmarek (2000)

WILLOW SPRINGS

Maple Lake - 95th East of Archer Road (95th Street and Wolf 11200 W.)

Numerous reports of various drowning's at this lake, including a man who had his head decapitated in a boating accident.

Activity - Strange lights are seen hovering and darting across the lake. There are no vehicle lights that could be causing this, since the nearest road on that side of the lake is far beyond the tree line. No explanation is available. Could this be a victim searching for its decapitated head?
FURTHER READING:
Haunted Illinois, by Troy Taylor (1999)

WORTH

Holy Sepulchre Cemetery - 6001 W. 111th St. (Austin 6000 W., 11100 S.)

Southside of Chicago's miracle child, Mary Alice Quinn resides here. Mary was fourteen years old when she died. She is buried in the Reilly grave (Section 7, a few graves behind the Capone marker) not far off the 111th Street entrance. The child is said to have cured people and is currently up for sainthood. Other graves that are worth to see include the former Mayor of Chicago Richard J. Daley (Section 19, on the NW corner), also the Grimes Sisters (Section 37, 21-8).

Activity - Reports of smelling roses around the Quinn grave. Many people trek to this site and leave offerings at her grave in hope of being cured. She had told her parents she wanted to come back after death to help people. (See also Willow Springs, Grimes Sisters.)

FURTHER READING:

Graveyards of Chicago, by Ursula Bielski and Matt Hucke (1999)

Windy City Ghosts, by Dale Kaczmarek (2000)

PALOS HILLS

Ghostly Lady - Intersection of 123rd & LaGrange Road (LaGrange Rd. 9300 W., 12300 S.)

Activity - A young woman's apparition has been reported to come out of the woods and then disappear right in front of the restaurants door. The women is said to come from the west side of the street and across the intersection. There was a report not far from this area of a nearby murder in the woods.

FURTHER READING:

Windy City Ghosts, by Dale Kaczmarek (2000)

Sacred Heart Cemetery - 101st Kean Ave. (Kean Ave. 9200 W., 10100 S.)

Information - Local teenagers referred to this as "Werewolf Run". A hairy wolf like man was spotted in the woods at this intersection many years ago. There was a fatal car accident in which a father and mother while killed, while their baby mysteriously was thrown from the car and survived. No explanation for both of these events has yet been made.

FURTHER READING:

Chicago's Street Guide to the Supernatural, by Richard Crowe (2000)

BURR RIDGE

Grimes Sisters - German Church Road, just west of 104th Avenue (German Church Rd. 8300 S.)

In 1957, this is the place where Barbara and Patricia Grimes bodies were dumped. The easiest way to find this location would be to take I-55 south, exit County Line Road south, take a left onto German Church Road. The first set of guardrails on the left side of the road is where the bodies had been found.

Activity - Phantom cars. Strange sounds of a car stopping, a door opening, and then taking off. Reports of

what looks like two girls bodies' lying in a ditch, then suddenly vanishes. Is this the gruesome events of that dreadful night being replayed? The murders still are unsolved. (See also Worth, Holy Sepulchre)
FURTHER READING:
Haunted Illinois, by Troy Taylor (1999)
Windy City Ghosts, by Dale Kaczmarek (2000)

Fairmount Hills Cemetery - 9100 S. Archer Road (Archer is a diagonal Street)

Activity - Police patrol this area regularly. The gates on this cemetery entrance are never closed, as if inviting strange events to happen here. A body of a woman was found beaten and strangled within the property. The "White" Mausoleum once stood atop this hill and has supposedly been heard playing music back from the early 1900's. An apparition has been reported hanging around this location at night. (Ed. note, the mausoleum was torn down strangely after the old Cavallone's changed ownership. What was the connection?)
FURTHER READING:
Windy City Ghosts, by Dale Kaczmarek (2000)

LAGRANGE
LaGrange Public Library - 10 W. Cossitt (LaGrange Rd. 0 E&W, Cossitt 300 S.

Activity - This current library sits on the site of a home where some children perished in a fire. The basement is the children's section, where many times

children's books have been found open on the floor. These books are found usually in the morning hours before the library opens for business. One of the children who perished in the fire, liked to read a certain book. Rumor has it the books that are found; always include that one special book. Also voices are heard late at night in the basement after closing hours.
FURTHER READING:
Chicago's Street Guide to the Supernatural, by Richard Crowe (2000)

HINSDALE
Hinsdale Animal Cemetery 6400 S. Bentley (Bentley 6400 S.)

Activity - Some people say that when their loved pets pass on they like to return just like humans do. There have been sightings of phantom animals throughout the cemetery.
FURTHER READING:
Windy City Ghosts, by Dale Kaczmarek (2000)

NORRIDGE
John Wayne Gacy Home - 8213 W. Summerdale Avenue (Summerdale Ave 5334 N.)

Information - This is now a renumbered private residence. John Wayne Gacy, the man who hid behind a clown's make-up. He would entertain kids at hospitals, and tried to basically be your neighborhood role model. In 1978, he confessed to the police he killed at least thirty boys and men, then buried majority of them in the crawl space of his basement. Nine victims were not identified. Gacy was eventually found guilty of killing thirty-three people. Though the building has been demolished, it didn't take long for the property to sell. The new owner, did rebuild a new house, and have a new address assigned. The question is, whether the bodies that were removed, do they rest in peace or haunt the property? Rumor has it that his body is buried in a family unmarked grave.

FURTHER READING:

The Man Who Killed Boys, by Clifford Linedecker (1980)

Killer Clowns, by Terry Sullivan and Peter Maiken (1983)

Buried Dreams, by Tim Cahill (1986)

WESTMONT

Clarendon Hills Cemetery - 6900 S. Cass Avenue (Cass Ave 1600 W, 6900 S.)

Activity - There are numerous events that take place here including screams within the cemetery late at night, possible satanic rituals performed here in the past, strange lights, mysterious apparitions, and a few unexplained deaths. A woman's body was found in a field within the cemetery, and a man's apparition has been reported staggering out of the cemetery toward the apartments covered in blood.

FURTHER READING:

Windy City Ghosts, by Dale Kaczmarek (2000)

Haunted Illinois, by Troy Taylor (1999)

DES PLAINES

Crash of Flight 191 - Near 320 W. Touhy Avenue (West of Mt. Prospect Rd., Touhy Ave. 7200 N.)

Activity - This is possibly the worst aviation crash in Chicago aviation history. The plane had taken off from O'Hare, encountered engine trouble and crashed. On board the plane were 258 passengers and 13 crewmembers. The animals that live in the trailer park are constantly barking for no apparent

reason. A man who seems to be smoldering and stinking of jet fuel has often been seen running around asking where to find a pay phone. Inside the airport, at the gate where the plane took off, a man has been spotted walking away from the pay phone only to disappear. There have been reports of people moaning and crying in the area of the crash. Some people have heard what sounds like a jet engine with a strange whine, then a sudden loud bang as if something crashed. Could this be the crash being replayed over and over like any tragic event?

FURTHER READING:
Windy City Ghosts, by Dale Kaczmarek (2000)

HICKORY HILLS
9500 S. Kean Avenue Intersection (Kean Av. 9200 W., 9500 S.)

Activity - At this apparent intersection numerous horses and riders have been killed. Before the stoplights were installed, riders would attempt to cross only to be struck by eastbound approaching vehicles. There have been numerous sightings of phantom horses with riders crossing this intersection. Horses have been known to be spooked as they approach this intersection.

FURTHER READING:
Haunted Illinois, by Troy Taylor (1999)
Windy City Ghosts, By Dale Kaczmarek (2000)

COUNTRY CLUB HILLS
I-57 Murders - I-57 & Flossmoor Road (I-57 Northbound lanes, Flossmoor Road 191st)

Activity - This is the area where a gruesome murder took place. An apparent accident was staged and a twenty five year old couple was brutally murdered. The bodies were not immediately discovered. There are reports of a couple seen on the side of the road, trying to flag down motorists in desperation. Local residents keep on the lookout while they travel through this area. One of the people who were charged in the murders actually had a run in with mass murderer John Wayne Gacy while

in prison.
FURTHER READING:
Windy City Ghosts, by Dale Kaczmarek (2000)

EVERGREEN PARK
Evergreen Cemetery - 8700 S. Kedzie (Kedzie 3200 W., 8700 S.)

Activity - A brunette ghost has been seen hitchhiking along the cemetery road on the Kedzie side. The other area where an event took place is around the bus stop at 88th St., on the cemetery side, where back in 1980 she had even got on a CTA bus only to vanish when the driver asked her for her fare.
FURTHER READING:
Windy City Ghosts, by Dale Kaczmarek (2000)

ALSIP
St. Casimir's Cemetery - 4401 W. 111th St. (Pulaski 4000 W.)

Activity - There have been reports of a strange man who is seen wearing a cape and having a ghostly white face with fangs, near the cemetery entrance. People have seen him while waiting at the light at Kostner and 111th street. He would just stand there and eventually would just vanish. Bike riders or people walking by report hearing a growling sound as though someone is trying to ward off intruders.
FURTHER READING:
Graveyards of Chicago, by Ursula Bielski and Matt Hucke

ELMHURST
Arlington Cemetery - Lake Street and Frontage Road (Lake St., County Line Rd.)

Activity - Reports have been made on a hitchhiker who apparently is dressed like a clown often seen along the exit ramp of North Avenue next to the cemetery. There seems to be no known explanation as to why this phenomenon is happening.

FURTHER READING:

Windy City Ghosts, by Dale Kaczmarek (2000)

STEGER
Calvary Cemetery -Steger Road and Western Avenue

Activity - This cemetery is south of Sauk Trail Woods Forest Preserve. If you turn east onto Steger Road from Western you be driving into an area that has no streetlights. Upon entering the residential area you be coming upon the cemetery entrance, this is the area where a young boy has been seen riding a bicycle. The apparition just rides across the two lanes of traffic without a care in the world. As motorists panic and swerve their car to avoid hitting the little boy on the bike, they eventually pull over to get out to finding no trace of anyone. Some have claimed to hit the apparition while others narrowly missed.

FURTHER READING:

Chicago's Street Guide to the Supernatural, by Richard Crowe (2000)

OAK BROOK
Peabody's Tomb - 31st and St. Pascal's (Rt. 83 also known as Kingery Rd., 3100 S.)

Information - This is the site where the Portiuncula Chapel marks the spot where on August 27, 1922 Frances Peabody apparently had a heart attack, fell and struck his head. He is buried beneath the chapel. Local legend has it that a body was encased in glass and on display in the chapel. As a display of manhood, teenage boys would have to sneak on the grounds at night and peer into the chapel window, looking for Peabody.

FURTHER READING:

Chicago Haunts, by Ursula Bielski (1998)

ROSEMONT
Allstate Arena -6920 N. Manheim Rd. (Manheim Rd is also Rt.45, Touhy 7200 N.)

Information - This building was known for years as the Rosemont Horizon. While the building was under construction the roof collapsed killing three workers. There are phantom noises throughout the building. Guards have heard footsteps behind them only to their surprise to turn around and find nobody there. There are reports of strange sounds of hammering being done when the building is closed for the night.

FURTHER READING:

Windy City Ghosts II, by Dale Kaczmarek (2001)

OAK PARK

Hephzibah Children's Home - 946 North Boulevard (Boulevard 2935 W.)

Activity - There was reports by employees and visitors that some sort of poltergeist effects have been going on at this children's home. Research was conducted and has been linked to an emotionally troubled adolescent, whom unconsciously was releasing some sort of psychokinetic energy. Could this be proof that the unconscious mind is actually in control?

FURTHER READING:

Windy City Ghosts, by Dale Kaczmarek (2000)

PARANORMAL RESEARCH ORGANIZATIONS

GHOST RESEARCH SOCIETY
P.O. Box 205
Oak Lawn, Il. 60454-0205
(708) 425-5163

WEB SITES

Ghost Research Society
www.ghostresearch.org

Parascience International
www.parascience.com

American Ghost Society
www.prairieghosts.com

Graveyards of Chicago
www.graveyards.com

Haunted Places Directory
www.haunted-places.com

The Ghost Society
http://pages.prodigy.net/ghostfish

The Ghost Club
www.ghostclub.org.uk

Richard Lindberg, Chicago Crime Historian
www.richardlindberg.net

Randy Liebeck, Investigator/Consultant
http://ghosthunter.Iwarp.com

Richard Senate
www.ghost-stalker.com

Loren Colemen, Fortean Investigator and Cryptozoologist
www.lorencoleman.com

Military Ghosts
www.militaryghosts.com

Fate Magazine
www.fatemag.com

Haunted Chicago
www.hauntedchicago.com

Paranormal Network
www.mindreader.com

Chicago Public Library
www.chipublib.org

Strange Magazine
www.strangemag.com

Find a Grave

www.findagrave.com

Visionary Living

www.visionaryliving.com

American Maps

www.creativesalesmaps.com

BIBLIOGRAPHY

Kaczmarek, Dale. Windy City Ghosts, Windy City Ghosts II.

Hauck, Dennis William. Haunted Places, the National Directory.

Hucke, Matt. Graveyards of Chicago.

Bielski, Ursula. Chicago Haunts, Graveyards of Chicago.

Taylor, Troy. Haunted Illinois.

Lindberg, Richard. Return to the Scene of the Crime.

Crowe, Richard. Chicago's Street Guide to the Supernatural.

Chicago Sun-Times newspaper

Chicago Tribune newspaper

Chicago Public Library

ABOUT THE AUTHOR

Jim Graczyk was born and raised in Chicago and throughout his life has been fascinated with local neighborhood tales, strange stories and especially with the promise of ghosts and the supernatural.

Although currently a full-time student, he is working on a second Bachelors Degree in Elementary Education and plans on becoming a teacher. Graczyk currently holds a Bachelors Degree in Psychology.

He is the Research Assistant with the Chicago-based group, Ghost Research Society. The Ghost Research Society was formed as a clearinghouse for reports of ghosts, hauntings, poltergeist and life after death encounters. The society members actively research and investigate all reports that come their way including private homes and businesses. The society also analyzes alleged spirit photographs, video and audiotapes that they come across form ordinary people or society members.

In addition to writing about haunted sites, Graczyk has written numerous articles for *Ghost of the Prairie Magazine* and has also appeared in a number of television shows and documentaries about ghosts. Those include Real Ghosthunters on the Discovery Channel and Basic Ghost Hunting by Video Hammer Productions.

He currently resides with is daughter, Rachel, in the southwest suburb's of Chicago.

INDEX

49th Street and Loomis, 52
95th Kean Avenue, 101
Acacia Park Cemetery, 80
Adolph Luetgert House, 79
Al Capone Grave, 48, 87
Al Capone Headquarters, 53
Allstate Arena, 104
Alonzi's Villa, 85
Arlington Cemetery, 103
Bachelors Grove Cemetery, 93
Bethania Cemetery, 91
Beverly Unitarian Church, 44
Bill Goat Tavern, 67
Biograph Theater, 70
Bleeding Stop Sign, 84
Bohemian National Cemetery, 74
Bregovy, Mary, 90
Bucktown Pub, 80
Burnham, Daniel, 75
Calvary Cemetery (Chicago), 73
Calvary Cemetery (Steger), 103
Captain H. Scheuenemann, 80,114
Cermak, Anton, 74
Chicago Transit Authority, 66
Chinatown, 55
Clarence Darrow Bridge, 49
Clarendon Hills Cemetery, 99
Clark Street Bridge, 59
Clark, Inez, 76
Comiskey, Charles, 73
Country House Restaurant, 86
Crash of Flight 191, 100
Daley, Richard J., 95
Darrow, Clarence, 49
Eastland Disaster, 31, 59, 74
El Train Wreck 1977, 66
Ethyl's Party, 56
Evergreen Cemetery, 102
Excalibur, 61
Fairmount Hills Cemetery, 97
Field Museum, 51
Field, Marshall, 75
Figure in the Window, 57
Firehouse Engine Co. 107, 45
Flight 191, 100
Former John Gacy Home, 98
Fort Dearborn, 26, 45
Frank Nitto's Suicide, 83, 87
Ghostly Lady, 95
Glessner House, 46
Glessner, John, 46, 76
Glowing Man of 67th Street, 52
Graceland Cemetery, 75
Green Hornet Collision, 54
Grimes Sisters, 17, 95, 96
Harpo Studio, 60
Haymarket Riots, 66
Hephzibah Children's Home, 105
Hines, Edward, 73
Hinsdale Animal Cemetery, 98

Holy Family Church, 50
Holy Sepulchre Cemetery, 95
Hooters Restaurant, 66
Hopkinson, Charles, 77
Hull House, 46
Hymie Weiss, 87
I-57 Murders, 101
Illinois Central Railroad, 52
Intersection Stop Sign, 84
Iroquois Theater, 12, 62
Italian Bride, 87
Jane Adams Hull House, 46
Jewish Waldheim Cemetery, 83
John Hancock Building, 63
John Hancock High School, 47
John Wayne Gacy, 98
Julia Buccola Peta, 87
Kaiser Hall, 50
Kelly, John, 73
Kimball, William, 75
Kwa Ma Rolas Totem Pole, 73
LaGrange Public Library, 97
LaSalle Hotel, 36
Lexington Hotel, 53
Lincoln Funeral Train, 56
Lourdes High School, 47
Maple Lake, 94
Marge's Pub, 78
Mary Bregovy, 90
Mary Alice Quinn, 95
McCarthy House, 53
McCormick, Cyrus, H., 75
Midlothian Turnpike, 94

Midway Crash Flight 533, 54
Moline House, 87
Monks Castle, 92
Morton College, 85
Mount Olivet Cemetery, 48
Mount Auburn Cemetery, 89
Mount Carmel Cemetery, 87
Mudgett, Herman Webster, 48
Murder Castle, 48
Nitti, Frank, 83, 87
O'Banion, Dion, 87
O'Hare Hilton, 81
O'Leary Barn, 64
O'Leary Grave, 48
Our Lady of Angels Memorial, 88
Our Lady of Angels, 4, 76, 88
Peabody's Tomb, 104
Peter Schuttler Mansion, 65
Pinkerton, Allan, 75
Pullman, George M., 75
Queen of Heaven Cemetery, 88
Quinn, Mary Alice, 95
Red Light Restaurant, 67
Red Lion Pub, 71
Resurrection Cemetery, 90
Rialto Theater, 89
Robinson Woods, 75
Rosehill Cemetery, 77
Rubloff Building, 65
Sacred Heart Cemetery, 96
Scheuenemann, Captain H, 80, 114
Sears, Richard W., 77

Seaweed Charlie, 73
Shedd, John G., 77
Showmen's Rest, 84
Smyth, John M., 73
St. Andrew's Pub, 72
St. Casmir Cemetery, 102
St. George's Church, 86
St. James Cemetery, 92
St. Rita Church, 49
St. Turbius, 47
St. Valentine's Day Massacre, 69
Stockyard Fire of 1910, 40, 55
Stockyards, 40
Strange Shape in the Window, 57

That Steak Joynt, 72
Tito's Restaurant, 56
Totem Pole, 73
Victorian House Antiques, 72
Village Commons, 84
Visitation Church, 53
Ward, Aaron Montgomery, 77
Water Tower, 62
Weiss, Hymie, 87
Werewolf Run, 96
Western Electric Employees, 74
Why Not Drive In, 91
Wincrest Nursing Home, 23, 79
Woodlawn Cemetery, 83

AUTHOR'S CUT

You've heard of the Director's Cut in a movie, well we at Ghost Research Society Press have what we call the Author's Cut. It is material that the author thought to include before the editors got their hands into the book. Included here in some way or form, the reader might come upon new or updated stories, pictures, emails or any type of correspondence.

THE CHRISTMAS TREE CAPTAIN

Everyone at some point in our lives believes in Santa, but for many people from the Chicagoland area there was an even a more special person they called "Captain Santa." Others called him by a name they knew in which he provided a service, which was the "Christmas Tree Captain." This "Captain Santa" was the warm-hearted Herman Schuenemann of the Rouse Simmons.

At a certain time of year, Captain Schuenemann would make a yearly voyage from Michigan's Upper Peninsula to Chicago with a load of freshly cut Christmas trees. Upon making his way into Chicago he would tie up along the SW Corner of the Clark Street Bridge. This was the place he even listed as his business address, the Northern Michigan Nursery.

The Northern Michigan Nursery came about at some point in Schuenemann's career after he gave up buying trees from suppliers and hired his own crew to go into the woods and cut trees. Schuenemann further eliminated the middleman by selling trees himself from the deck of his ship instead of to store owners. Time eventually took its toll and by 1912 the railroads and highways were making these ships obsolete.

In 1912, he owned 240 acres in upper Michigan. Every voyage was a make-or-break adventure. Failure to bring back trees would leave him penniless, but success meant doubling or tripling his income between Thanksgiving and Christmas. This years holiday season and weather were going to be different; a storm already had took its toll on the Great Lakes shippers.

The worst snowstorm in a century had blasted the lakes for four days before Thanksgiving, destroying 10 large freighters and littering the shoreline with debris. Four hundred seamen already lost their lives in these disastrous days.

Meanwhile Captain Schuenemann was realizing he could turn a disaster into profit. The snow had buried tree farms in Wisconsin and Michigan. Chicago tree merchants were desperate for trees. Captain Schuenemann was happy to deliver!

At the Thompson Harbor, Michigan trees were being crammed into every available space on the Rouse Simmons. It was well into the evening when the Captain ordered more bundles of trees tied on board the deck, row upon row. The schooner sagged under the weight of her fragrant cargo. Schuenemann expected this to be his most profitable year he had ever made.

Despite stormy weather, the Rouse Simmons set sail at noon on November 22, 1912. As the Rouse Simmons swung west-southwest heading toward Chicago she became engulfed in deadly winds of 60 miles per hour. As fate would have it, the violent wind had changed suddenly, producing a furious snowstorm and an incredible drop in temperature. A thick blanket of ice quickly thickened as the unrelenting waves pounded the ship. Battered hatch covers could no longer prevent water from entering the hold where it quickly turned into ice on the trees.

From the station tower at Sturgeon Bay, Wisconsin, men sighted the Rouse Simmons flying distress signals as she continued to move low in the water, driven along by the force of the gale. A rescue team was dispatched in an attempt intercept the suffering schooner.

Visibility was difficult and a two hour search proving to be unsuccessful. Just then there was a break in the snowstorm and the ship sighted. From what men could make of it, the ship was barely afloat and resembled a floating piece of ice. Rescuers desperately moved full steam ahead and blinding snow again made it impossible to see the schooner. The Rouse Simmons vanished from sight and was never seen again.

Eventually divers found the wreck of the Rouse Simmons in 165 feet of water off the coast of Two Rivers Wisconsin. Some of the historic ship was salvaged for display, which included the anchor that stands today at the entrance to the Milwaukee Yacht Club. Also the schooner's wheel can be found at the Rogers Street Fishing Village in Two Rivers, Wisconsin. Though Captain Schuenemann's body was never recovered, his wife is buried in Acacia Cemetery, Section Westaria, 21-4. Strangely the grave is said to produce the scent of fresh cut spruce and balsam. (Acacia Cemetery is located in Chicago, 7800 W. Irving Park Road.)

Captain Schuenemann and the Rouse Simmons.

COMING SOON FROM THE GHOST RESEARCH SOCIETY PRESS

FIELD GUIDE TO SPIRIT PHOTOGRAPHY
The Essential Guide to Cameras in Paranormal Research
By Dale Kaczmarek

FIELD GUIDE TO THE LAND OF LINCOLN
Ghostly Tales & Haunted Sites from across the State of Illinois
By Jim Graczyk

And don't Miss Any Books in the Series by
Visiting Our Website at:
http://www.ghostguides.com

Or Visit the Ghost Research Society Press at:
http://www.ghostresearch.org/press.html

Printed in the United States
109038LV00003B/162/A